FAILING THE INTERNALLY DISPLACED

The UNDP Displaced Persons Program in Kenya

Human Rights Watch/Africa

Human Rights Watch
New York · Washington · London · Brussels

ISBN 1-56432-212-2
Library of Congress Catalog Card Number: 97-72316

Human Rights Watch/Africa
Human Rights Watch/Africa was established in 1988 to monitor and promote the observance of internationally recognized human rights in sub-Saharan Africa. Peter Takirambudde is the executive director; Janet Fleischman is the Washington director; Suliman Ali Baldo is the senior researcher; Alex Vines is the research associate; Bronwen Manby and Binaifer Nowrojee are counsels; Ariana Pearlroth and Juliet Wilson are associates; and Alison DesForges is a consultant. William Carmichael is the chair of the advisory committee and Alice Brown is the vice chair.

Addresses for Human Rights Watch
485 Fifth Avenue, New York, NY 10017-6104
Tel: (212) 972-8400, Fax: (212) 972-0905, E-mail: hrwnyc@hrw.org

1522 K Street, N.W., #910, Washington, DC 20005-1202
Tel: (202) 371-6592, Fax: (202) 371-0124, E-mail: hrwdc@hrw.org

33 Islington High Street, N1 9LH London, UK
Tel: (171) 713-1995, Fax: (171) 713-1800, E-mail: hrwatchuk@gn.apc.org

15 Rue Van Campenhout, 1000 Brussels, Belgium
Tel: (2) 732-2009, Fax: (2) 732-0471, E-mail: hrwatcheu@gn.apc.org

Web Site Address: http://www.hrw.org
Gopher Address://gopher.humanrights.org:5000/11/int/hrw
Listserv address: To subscribe to the list, send an e-mail message to majordomo@igc.apc.org with "subscribe hrw-news" in the body of the message (leave the subject line blank).

HUMAN RIGHTS WATCH

Human Rights Watch conducts regular, systematic investigations of human rights abuses in some seventy countries around the world. Our reputation for timely, reliable disclosures has made us an essential source of information for those concerned with human rights. We address the human rights practices of governments of all political stripes, of all geopolitical alignments, and of all ethnic and religious persuasions. Human Rights Watch defends freedom of thought and expression, due process and equal protection of the law, and a vigorous civil society; we document and denounce murders, disappearances, torture, arbitrary imprisonment, discrimination, and other abuses of internationally recognized human rights. Our goal is to hold governments accountable if they transgress the rights of their people.

Human Rights Watch began in 1978 with the founding of its Helsinki division. Today, it includes five divisions covering Africa, the Americas, Asia, the Middle East, as well as the signatories of the Helsinki accords. It also includes three collaborative projects on arms transfers, children's rights, and women's rights. It maintains offices in New York, Washington, Los Angeles, London, Brussels, Moscow, Dushanbe, Rio de Janeiro, and Hong Kong. Human Rights Watch is an independent, nongovernmental organization, supported by contributions from private individuals and foundations worldwide. It accepts no government funds, directly or indirectly.

The staff includes Kenneth Roth, executive director; Michele Alexander, development director; Cynthia Brown, program director; Barbara Guglielmo, finance and administration director; Robert Kimzey, publications director; Jeri Laber, special advisor; Lotte Leicht, Brussels office director; Susan Osnos, communications director; Jemera Rone, counsel; Wilder Tayler, general counsel; and Joanna Weschler, United Nations representative.

The regional directors of Human Rights Watch are Peter Takirambudde, Africa; José Miguel Vivanco, Americas; Sidney Jones, Asia; Holly Cartner, Helsinki; and Eric Goldstein, Middle East (acting). The project directors are Joost R. Hiltermann, Arms Project; Lois Whitman, Children's Rights Project; and Dorothy Q. Thomas, Women's Rights Project.

The members of the board of directors are Robert L. Bernstein, chair; Adrian W. DeWind, vice chair; Roland Algrant, Lisa Anderson, William Carmichael, Dorothy Cullman, Gina Despres, Irene Diamond, Fiona Druckenmiller, Edith Everett, Jonathan Fanton, James C. Goodale, Jack Greenberg, Vartan Gregorian, Alice H. Henkin, Stephen L. Kass, Marina Pinto Kaufman, Bruce Klatsky, Harold Hongju Koh, Alexander MacGregor, Josh Mailman, Samuel K. Murumba, Andrew Nathan, Jane Olson, Peter Osnos, Kathleen Peratis, Bruce Rabb, Sigrid Rausing, Anita Roddick, Orville Schell, Sid Sheinberg, Gary G. Sick, Malcolm Smith, Domna Stanton, Maureen White, and Maya Wiley.

ABBREVIATIONS AND ACRONYMS

D.C.	District Commissioner
DHA	Department of Humanitarian Affairs
D.O.	District Officer
ECOSOC	U.N. Economic and Social Council
E.U.	European Union
FERA	February the Eighteenth Resistance Army
FORD	Forum for the Restoration of Democracy
IASC	Inter-Agency Standing Committee
ICCPR	International Covenant on Civil and Political Rights
ICESCR	International Covenant on Economic, Social and Cultural Rights
KADU	Kenya African Democratic Union
KANU	Kenya African National Union
Kshs.	Kenya shilling [U.S.$1 = Kshs.55 in this report]
Quips	Quick Impact Projects
NCCK	National Council of Churches of Kenya
NCDP	National Committee for Displaced Persons
NGO	Nongovernmental organization
P.C.	Provincial Commissioner
U.N.	United Nations
UNDP	U.N. Development Program
UNHCR	Office of the U.N. High Commissioner for Refugees
UNICEF	U.N. Children's Fund
UNIFEM	U.N. Development Fund for Women
U.S.	United States
U.K	United Kingdom
WFP	World Food Program
WHO	World Health Organization
WPCC	Western Province Coordinating Committee

CONTENTS

PREFACE

Human Rights Watch/Africa has closely followed the situation of the internally displaced in Kenya since the inception of the "ethnic" violence in 1991 that caused the displacement of an estimated 300,000 persons. In 1993, we published a book-length report entitled *Divide and Rule: State-Sponsored Ethnic Violence in Kenya*, which documented the plight of those displaced by the violence and the Kenyan government's role in instigating the violence for political purposes. In 1994 and 1995, Human Rights Watch/Africa published updates documenting ongoing government harassment, intimidation and violence occurring against the displaced.

In July and August 1996, Human Rights Watch/Africa returned to Kenya to interview internally displaced persons and others. The mission traveled through seven districts: Bungoma, Mt. Elgon, Kisumu, Nakuru, Nandi, Trans Nzoia and Uasin Gishu. Human Rights Watch/Africa also visited Maela camp, the site of forced government dispersals more than two years ago, and interviewed a number of the displaced who were still there or who had returned to the site. Some of those interviewed had been displaced since the violence began more than five years ago. Human Rights Watch/Africa also interviewed a number of formerly displaced persons who had returned to their land or had settled elsewhere.

Although this report provides an update on the current situation of the internally displaced in Kenya, it is primarily an examination of the efforts of the international community to fulfill its human rights obligations, under the U.N. Charter, to the internally displaced. This report demonstrates the necessity of centrally incorporating human rights and protection concerns from the outset in programs for the internally displaced. The report examines a program for the internally displaced administered by the development arm of the United Nations (U.N.), the United Nations Development Program (UNDP), in Kenya between 1993 to 1995. Although the program was ended in September 1995, this report offers an opportunity for the U.N., and UNDP in particular, to evaluate the lessons of the Kenyan experience in order to strengthen future programs. It is our hope that this report will contribute toward a stronger international framework for assistance and protection to the internally displaced.

Prior to publication, Human Rights Watch/Africa shared sections of the draft report with UNDP in order to provide it with an opportunity to reflect its perspective on the findings of the report. On March 26, 1997, Human Rights Watch/Africa met with William Paton, Migration and Resettlement Specialist, and Edmund Cain, Director, Emergency Response Division, and provided UNDP with relevant sections of the draft report. On April 28, 1997, Human Rights Watch/Africa received a response from UNDP Administrator James Gustave Speth welcoming an opportunity to discuss the findings of the report further. UNDP also provided Human Rights Watch/Africa with an eight-page commentary on the draft report stating that the comments "attempt to set the record straight on the most serious, if not all, of the assertions which we believe to be wrong." UNDP's considered response to the draft report was appreciated and taken into account in finalizing the report. Human Rights Watch/Africa has, as best as possible, incorporated UNDP's comments into the final report. Accordingly, the page numbers of the Human Rights Watch/Africa draft report referred to in the UNDP comments no longer correspond. The full text of UNDP's comments have been attached as an appendix to the report.

This report was written by Binaifer Nowrojee, Counsel with Human Rights Watch/Africa. It was edited by Peter Takirambudde, Executive Director of Human Rights Watch/Africa; Joanna Weschler, U.N. Representative of Human Rights Watch; Dinah PoKempner, Deputy General Counsel of Human Rights Watch; and Jeri Laber, Senior Advisor with Human Rights Watch. Invaluable production assistance was provided by Ariana Pearlroth and Juliet Wilson, Associates with Human Rights Watch/Africa.

Maela Camp, 1994.
Photograph courtesy of *Daily Nation*, Nation Newspaper, Ltd., Nairobi, Kenya.

1. SUMMARY

It is only in recent years that the U.N., through a number of its agencies, has begun to improve its capacity to provide humanitarian assistance, protection and reintegration[1] support to the escalating numbers of internally displaced worldwide. The plight of the internally displaced within their country has gone largely unaddressed by the international community because primary responsibility for their safety and assistance needs lies with their own government. The absence of an internationally recognized legal status, the assertion of sovereignty by national governments, and the lack of any clear mechanism for international assistance have further contributed to a lower level of international protection than comparably situated refugees who have crossed an international border. However, the international community is increasingly recognizing that it is legally entitled to provide such assistance where governments are unable or unwilling to fulfill their commitments under international law. Since there is no one agency within the U.N. with overall responsibility for the internally displaced, a number of different U.N. agencies have been designated on an *ad hoc* basis by the secretary-general to administer these programs, including the Office of the High Commissioner for Refugees (UNHCR) and UNDP among others.

This development, while commendable and long overdue, has not been without the inevitable growing pains that occur as an institution evolves to address new areas. An examination of the current approach reveals an uneven, limited, and, in many cases, unsatisfactory international response that is dependent on the institution selected to deal with the issue. A major impediment to the effective implementation of international programs—by the variety of U.N. agencies with widely differing mandates—is that this expansion has not been accompanied by the requisite capacity-building, within and between these agencies, to best meet the needs of the internally displaced. This has particular relevance in the areas of human rights and protection, which are a dimension of internal displacement.

In the face of a changing world, most U.N. agencies administering programs to the displaced are treading on difficult, and often unknown, territory.

---

[1] In this report, the word reintegration is used to refer to long-term solutions in which the displaced are voluntarily returned to their homes or are voluntarily and permanently relocated elsewhere. The term resettlement is also used by people or documents cited in this report to mean the same thing. However, resettlement has a distinct and different connotation in the refugee context, referring specifically to refugees who are permanently relocated to a third country. In order to avoid any such connotation, Human Rights Watch/Africa has, as much as possible, used the word reintegration.

Human Rights Watch/Africa does not underestimate the logistical and political difficulties that will often be faced in such a situation. The needs of the internally displaced span a wide range from the immediate requirements of food, shelter and protection from violence, to longer-term considerations that can resolve underlying tensions and restore them to their homes and livelihoods. International programs for the internally displaced inevitably must include emergency relief assistance, protection, prevention and development components.

Human rights concerns are integral to all the components of a program to assist the internally displaced. Often, human rights violations cause the displacement and, not surprisingly, human rights and justice issues are at the core of finding lasting solutions that can allow the internally displaced to return to their land or be reintegrated elsewhere. Protection encompasses both security of person and property, as well as guarantees of legal protection and redress for rights abuses. Accordingly, human rights promotion and protection work must be a central component of international programs for the internally displaced. The cost of ignoring human rights and protection concerns will be the resulting failure to reach lasting solutions.

Under the U.N. Charter, the duty to promote and protect human rights is within the mandate of all U.N. agencies. Human Rights Watch/Africa recognizes that ultimate responsibility for providing these assurances to the internally displaced lies with the government. We are not advocating that U.N. agencies replace governments nor that they transform themselves into policing or investigative bodies. Rather, in situations of reintegration where abuses are systematic, it is incumbent on the implementing U.N. agency to be prepared to assume active responsibility for being a protector and advocate for the displaced. Among other things, this includes a willingness to vigorously and publicly protest abuses against the displaced, and to put into place minimum conditions for operation that ensure fundamental human rights and protection considerations are met.

In accepting that human rights is part of the U.N.'s mandate, it is not enough for U.N. agencies to make oblique or weak policy references as to the importance of incorporating human rights into emergency-type programs. U.N. agencies also cannot relinquish all responsibility for human rights to the U.N.'s Centre for Human Rights. What is required are tangible operating procedures, guidelines, and training to ensure that all staff have the necessary expertise and institutional support to take on the tasks of confronting abusive or uncooperative authorities and creating the secure environment required for reintegration to occur. Human rights and protection issues must be up front and central to the administration of programs for the internally displaced, not peripheral or expendable. It is not enough to include human rights marginally, and it is unacceptable to compromise human rights concerns when necessary to secure other operational goals.

UNDP, the U.N.'s development arm, is increasingly administering reintegration programs for the internally displaced. Like other U.N. agencies, UNDP is grappling with the difficult task of how best to design and implement programs that can find lasting solutions for internally displaced people to return home. UNDP has a broadly defined mandate to promote sustainable development. Its work has been traditionally limited to non-emergency situations in which the agency works closely with the government to implement development programs. Gradually, UNDP is shifting from its traditional approach to contribute in conflict situations where it can "bridge relief with development." UNDP's resident representatives based in the field are increasingly being designated to coordinate and lead programs for the internally displaced. With its expansion into emergency-type programs, including reintegration programs for the internally displaced, UNDP is being challenged to stretch its traditional capacity to address the operational challenges posed by such situations.

UNDP's recent policy documents recognize and acknowledge that human rights falls within the ambit of its development mandate and is critical to the success of emergency programs. This fact was reinforced in a statement by the U.N. Secretary-General Kofi Annan shortly after taking office in which he affirmed that human rights issues constituted a part of development work.[2] Although human rights functions have not been an established feature of its traditional work, UNDP has formally acknowledged that its mandate and its programs for the internally displaced must incorporate the issues of governance, social justice, human rights and land tenure. In fact, a reintegration program that UNDP implemented in Central America between 1989 and 1995 was considered a success in large part because UNDP made human rights a central component of that program.

However, UNDP has remained ambivalent about its recognition that human rights and protection are essential to the success of its emergency programs. UNDP has yet to take the next step to fully incorporate these components in tangible and consistent ways into its own operating procedures. The lessons and expertise of the Central American reintegration program were not translated into UNDP's Kenyan program. UNDP also appears unwilling or unprepared to fully address the difficulties that must accompany the task of defending and helping

---

[2]"UN Reform: The First Six Weeks," Statement by Kofi Annan, U.N. Secretary-General, New York, February 13, 1997.

internally displaced persons find lasting solutions, even in the face of hostile or uncooperative governments. If UNDP is to administer programs for the internally displaced, it must be willing to strengthen its capacity to provide human rights protection as well as be willing to adopt a vigorous advocacy approach against government actions that undermine reintegration. Reintegration and sustainable development cannot succeed in a context of insecurity, abuse and fear.

Human Rights Watch/Africa acknowledges at the outset the difficult role UNDP is called on to play in internally displaced situations, particularly in the face of complex political and social environments. We do not seek to downplay the challenges that U.N. staff face in the field, nor do we overlook the fact that such programs cannot be conducted effectively without the active involvement of the government or controlling authority. Presented with these real constraints, programs for the internally displaced often have to be conducted in politically-charged environments where human rights standards have been eroded. As a result, adequate preparation and training to tackle the human rights and protection issues remains all the more important. The correct approach to, and inclusion of, strong human rights and protection components in UNDP's internally displaced programs are vital to successful long-term reintegration.

In this context, it is particularly valuable to examine closely the UNDP Displaced Persons Program in Kenya which was administered between 1993 to 1995 in order to reintegrate an estimated 300,000 persons displaced by "ethnic" violence. Human Rights Watch/Africa has taken the trouble to revisit this program several years later because it contains some valuable lessons for UNDP that, if acted upon by UNDP, can improve its implementation of programs for the internally displaced. As far as internally displaced situations go, the Kenyan situation posed the sorts of challenges frequently encountered in these situations. Violence and rights abuses instigated by the government had caused the displacement, and, during the program, UNDP faced predictable constraints in its operations because of government actions hostile to genuine assistance and protection efforts.

The UNDP program in Kenya had tremendous potential which was never fulfilled. The general consensus about the UNDP Displaced Persons Program in Kenya—among local and international NGOs, international medical and relief groups, diplomats and even some UNDP employees who worked on the program—is that UNDP's record fell far short of what it could, and should, have been. Certain aspects of the program could have been handled better. As a result, thousands still remained displaced when the program ended, and the key issues underlying the displacement went unaddressed.

Amid the mixed results, there were a number of missed opportunities where UNDP could have made significant contributions. In assessing this program, Human Rights Watch/Africa in no way seeks to minimize the achievements of this program that facilitated the return of thousands. These figures are not insignificant, given the lack of real political change in Kenya. UNDP deserves full credit where it enabled and facilitated return. However, using figures of the reintegrated alone as a measure of success overlooks fundamental questions that must be an integral part of any assessment of a reintegration program: Have the conditions that created this displacement been addressed? Have the injustices and hostility caused by the violence and displacement been redressed? Is this society better able to prevent a recurrence of the problems that caused the displacement? If UNDP's aim was only to provide relief assistance to the displaced until some could go home and nothing more, then the agency can view this program as a success. If, however, the aim was, as stated, "the reintegration of displaced populations into local communities, prevention of renewed tensions and promotion of the process of reconciliation," then UNDP did not reach its own goals in fundamental ways.

The internal displacement that led to the creation of the UNDP Displaced Persons Program in Kenya began in 1991 after the Kenyan government was forced to concede to a multiparty system. In response, President Daniel arap Moi and his inner circle adopted a calculated policy against ethnic groups associated with the political opposition. In spite of Moi's pronouncements, the violence was not a spontaneous reaction to the reintroduction of multiparty politics. The government unleashed terror, provoked displacement, and expelled certain ethnic groups *en masse* from their long-time homes and communities in Nyanza, Western and Rift Valley Provinces for political and economic gain. This was particularly true for the Rift Valley Province which hosts the largest number of parliamentary seats and some of the most fertile land in the country. The government capitalized on unaddressed and competing land ownership issues dating from the colonial period between those pastoral groups, such as the Kalenjin and Maasai, who were ousted from land by British settlers and the agricultural laborers who subsequently settled on the land after independence. Many of these farms were at the center of the ethnic clashes, as they came to be known.

By 1993, Human Rights Watch/Africa estimated that 1,500 people had died in the clashes, and that some 300,000 were internally displaced. Of those displaced, an estimated 75 percent were children. The clashes pitted members of President Moi's small Kalenjin group and the Maasai, against the larger Kikuyu, Luhya and Luo ethnic groups. Kikuyu, Luhya and Luo-owned farms were attacked by organized groups of Kalenjin or Maasai "warriors" armed with traditional weapons such as bows and arrows. It was subsequently found that ruling party officials had paid some attackers a fee for each house burned and person killed, and that government vehicles had been used to transport the attackers. Security forces often stood by in the course of an attack, and appeals for protection went unheeded. By contrast, counter attacks against the Kalenjin or Maasai were usually more disorganized in character, and not as effective in driving people off their land. The great majority of those displaced were members of the Kikuyu Luhya and Luo ethnic groups from the Rift Valley, Western and Nyanza Provinces. Following a 1992 election win by President Moi and his ruling party the frequency of the attacks diminished steadily, but periodic incidents continued. Meanwhile, those displaced by the attacks fled to nearby churches, market centers, or abandoned buildings. Largely ignored by the government, they congregated in squalid conditions, receiving assistance largely from the churches and local nongovernmental organizations (NGOs).

In 1993, UNDP took commendable initiative to create a reconciliation and reintegration program for those displaced from the "ethnic" clashes. The stated objective of the proposed U.S.$20 million Programme for Displaced Persons was "the reintegration of displaced populations into local communities, prevention of renewed tensions and promotion of the process of reconciliation." The program was implemented jointly with the government. The program plan was based largely on two reports, known as the Rogge Reports, after the author. The first Rogge report, written in 1993, identified three groups of the displaced: those who had returned and were in the process of rehabilitating their homes and farms; those who were commuting to their farms to cultivate, but were not able or willing to return because of the perception or experience of continued insecurity; and those who would probably never be able to return because the remaining residents were emphatic about never allowing members of any other ethnic group to reclaim their land or because they were squatters with no legal claim to return.

The first Rogge report provided a sound and well-conceived proposal for action that included short-term relief assistance needs; medium-term needs for general development initiatives including the rehabilitation of destroyed institutions, reconciliation seminars, employment training, and regularization of the land tenure system; and long-term protection and security issues which, the report stressed, were paramount to the program's success.

By the time the UNDP program began, levels of violence had diminished significantly, and reintegration had begun to occur in some areas, particularly Nyanza and Western Province. However, at the same time, the government steadily undermined reintegration through active obstruction of reintegration efforts on some fronts and inaction on others. During the UNDP program, and since, there was no government commitment to reverse the damage that had been caused, and to restore the displaced to their lost land and livelihood without regard for ethnicity.

Even while progress was made in alleviating the emergency food and material assistance needs in the first year of the UNDP program and some reintegration occurred, a climate of mistrust and insecurity persisted in many parts of the Rift Valley. Numerous difficulties remained largely due to government resistance to full reintegration, and a lack of political will to restore security, to redress past and continuing injustices against the displaced, and to find lasting solutions particularly with regard to land reform. The Kenyan government continued to harass and intimidate the displaced after they were driven from their land. The government brought charges against critics of the government's policies towards the displaced, while at the same time it allowed the instigators and perpetrators of the violence to enjoy complete impunity. Where the displaced were congregated in groups that could attract negative attention, they were dispersed with threats or force by local government officials, often without regard for their safety and with no alternative accommodation. Those assisting the displaced or journalists attempting to report on the plight of the displaced were sometimes denied access to certain areas, arrested for short periods or harassed. If reintegration occurred, it was usually due to the efforts of the communities themselves or because a local government official quietly acted on personal initiative. In the more contentious areas, where Kalenjin and Maasai residents had vowed not to permit the displaced to return, or where local or national government leaders obstructed reintegration, no steps were taken by the government to restore the rule of law. Most importantly, the government took no action to work with UNDP to seek long-term solutions for redress and prevention, particularly in regard to the issue of land registration and tenure.

In the face of this largely predictable resistance from government quarters, UNDP appeared unprepared and unqualified to deal with the rights and protection implications that this raised. The manner in which the program was initially structured did not put into place safeguards to minimize government control or manipulation of the program. Instead of addressing the key impediments to lasting change, UNDP ignored the political, human rights, and development dimensions of the displacement. Building its approach on experience acquired previously through a drought alleviation program, UNDP proceeded as if all that was necessary was to provide relief supplies to enable people to return—while doing nothing more than acknowledging the political causes of the displacement and the attendant human rights violations that needed to be addressed. Also, based on its usual working approach, UNDP partnered itself closely with the government. Many of the issues that the Rogge reports identified as fundamental were disregarded in the implementation of the program. Where UNDP encountered government resistance to addressing an issue, such as human rights violations or land law reform, the agency's approach was to retreat rather than to press for these fundamental changes to be made. The narrow perspective adopted by UNDP resulted in a program that ignored issues responsible for the humanitarian crisis in Kenya which were key to finding lasting solutions.

Initially, UNDP did not secure any written commitment from the government to maintain security and to bind it to provide basic minimum conditions such as free access to the displaced, safeguards for the physical security and basic human rights of the displaced, and the free passage of humanitarian assistance. The lack of an operating agreement allowed the Kenyan government to continue to evade its responsibilities, while at the same time it was able to use the threat of ending access to silence UNDP. UNDP did create some successful national and local fora to bring together government officials, NGOs, community representatives and UNDP. However, these efforts, while bringing some pressure to bear on the government, were still not a sufficient replacement for a written agreement.

UNDP sought to remedy the lack of a formal working agreement by trying to work closely with the government and to provide positive incentives for the government to cooperate. This entailed downplaying human rights abuses as the acts of individuals in the government rather than the responsibility of the government. There were a wide variety of past and ongoing human rights abuses whose remedies were integral to finding lasting solutions. These included the denial of basic human rights to the displaced; the harassment, intimidation and forced dispersals of the displaced; the government's complete refusal to hold the perpetrators and inciters of the violence accountable; and the expropriation of the land owned by the displaced with a view to consolidating the new ethnic order of land distribution that had been imposed by the violence. Yet human rights monitoring and advocacy to protect the displaced were not a part of the program. UNDP staff tended to avoid any public denunciation of the abuses on the grounds that quiet representations would be more effective and would allow UNDP to secure various operational goals. The lack of any formal reporting requirement on these issues by UNDP in New York further reinforced the silence on human rights violations.

Protection of the physical safety of the internally displaced was as crucial to reintegration as relief assistance. Protection issues with the displaced in Kenya came up both with regard to ensuring physical security from threats of coercion and violence and the longer-term issue of defending legal rights that were violated by those responsible for the displacement. Although the provision of security is ultimately the responsibility of the government, UNDP had a major role to play in making protection concerns a priority with the Kenyan government. However, UNDP viewed this role as being too "political." While there was talk by UNDP of the need to create an enabling environment, no effort was made to promulgate articulated standards for the government or to protest government abuse effectively. UNDP never worked with the security forces and local administration to provide training on rights and legal responsibilities, nor did it seek to protect the legal rights of the displaced.

As a result of this approach, public statements by UNDP continually put forward positions that only reflected or exaggerated the positive developments, and ignored or downplayed government abuses against the displaced and other measures designed to perpetuate the new ethnic alignment in the regions from which the displaced were driven. The second Rogge report, published at the mid-point of the program in 1994, contributed to the impression that reintegration was largely proceeding with government cooperation, as did a 1994 visit to Kenya by Administrator Gustave Speth who publicly praised the Moi government for "moving to reconcile tribal differences." Mr. Speth made no mention of the continued threats or actual violence against the displaced, forced dispersals, the destruction of camp sites by administration police, or government harassment of those assisting the displaced. UNDP continually deflected international and local criticism of the government's human rights record toward the displaced. Based on UNDP's public gloss of the program, the Kenyan government was able to reassure donors and investors that it was taking steps to reintegrate the displaced. This, in turn, led to a widespread NGO suspicion that UNDP was hand-in-glove with the government.

UNDP also decided not to address the issue of accountability for past abuses—and government policies—which had caused the displacement, on the rationale that societies have to come to terms with their tragic pasts in their own way. UNDP continually downplayed the need for accountability, portraying the problem as one without victims and aggressors, but only communities that needed to be reconciled. However, in a situation where people had lost their families and homes, accountability and an acknowledgment of the wrong done to them, was a critical stepping stone to lasting reconciliation.

Throughout the program, the government was able to evade its responsibility to reintegrate by forcibly dispersing identifiable groups of displaced people. Since UNDP never prioritized data collection, UNDP was helpless to remedy the situation because it had not done a count or registered names. Additionally, at the mid-point of the program, NGOs working with the displaced accused UNDP of using the lack of data to inflate the estimates of the reintegrated in order to put the best face on its program.

The lack of any mechanisms within the program structure to prevent government abuse and manipulation, and UNDP's unwillingness to publicly raise concerns about these issues, alienated two strong allies: the international donor community and the local NGO community. Both groups have been a powerful force in calling for an end to human rights violations in Kenya. As a result of their efforts, significant improvements have occurred in the past decade. Yet, there was not a close partnership by UNDP with these sectors. As the program progressed, donors became more wary of committing funding to a program they saw to be increasingly compromised by UNDP's perceived acquiescence to government abuses. Eventually, some donors even withheld funding they had previously pledged.

This unfortunate situation was further aggravated by generally poorly managed NGO relations. UNDP did not support the work of other agencies or serve as a vigorous advocate to end the harassment of NGO staff. In Western Province, UNDP inadvertently undermined NGO efforts through its efforts to direct a regional committee to such an extent that when UNDP ended the program, the local initiatives were weaker than they had been before. An assessment report of Western Province, commissioned by UNDP itself, concluded that UNDP had "hijacked" the process, and "[i]n the end, their [UNDP's] whole participation was judged as a failure by all the actors on the ground."

Fraudulent land transfers or pressured land sales continued throughout the UNDP program, further disenfranchising Kikuyus, Luos and Luhyas, particularly in the Rift Valley Province. This aspect of reintegration was ironically the one UNDP was best suited to deal with—long-term development. Finding lasting solutions to the problem of internal displacement requires attention to the root causes. In Kenya, these were the unresolved land tenure issues arising from the colonial period which was manipulated by Kenya's government for political ends. The "ethnic" violence had furthered this process. Yet, UNDP did not prioritize this politically thorny issue in order to push the Kenyan government toward a land law reform program. As a result, land continues to be fraudulently transferred, illegally occupied, and sold or exchanged unfairly, further disempowering the internally displaced and contributing to the removal of certain ethnic groups from the Rift Valley Province up to today.

Ultimately, the manner in which the program was administered resulted in the greatest attention being placed on that part of the program that was relatively the easiest and least politically controversial to administer—the relief part—and a neglect of protection, human rights, and long-term needs, which would have required UNDP to adopt a more critical advocacy role in relation to the Kenyan government. In the end, UNDP was immobilized. UNDP was neither able to address the long-term developmental issues for reintegration which it had the expertise to do, nor was it able to channel sufficient pressure on the government where needed because it lacked the experience and political will.

The final blow to the flagging program was the forced expulsion of some 2,000 Kikuyu from Maela camp, who were trucked out of the camp after a police raid in the middle of the night on December 24, 1994, without the knowledge of UNDP, and dumped at three sites in their "ancestral" home of Central Province. A few days later, many of the same people were subjected to a second round of police raids, as the government tried to disperse them as quickly as possible. For the first time, UNDP became an outspoken advocate of the displaced, calling on the government and the world to stop these abuses. By that time, however, UNDP's position was so compromised, it was in no position to mobilize donor and NGO support. Despite assurances from UNDP that it would protect those who had been displaced from Maela, UNDP never returned them to Maela, nor did the agency succeed in pressuring the government to punish the responsible officials. At one point, UNDP's resident representative to Kenya characterized the forced dispersal as a "temporary hiccup" in the program, in a bid to urge donors and others not to allow this incident to detract from the positive contributions of the program. Moreover, because UNDP had such poor NGO relations and a record of praising the government, UNDP became a target of blame for the Maela camp incident, irreparably damaging its image and credibility in Kenya. The Maela incident brought the UNDP Displaced Persons Program in Kenya to a halt. It was formally ended in November 1995.

To date, the Kenyan government has condoned the illegal occupation of land by its political supporters and the continued displacement of thousands of its citizens from ethnic groups that are perceived to support the political opposition. The government has taken the minimum steps necessary to allay public criticism of its policies of ethnic persecution and discrimination. Although some of its actions have promoted reintegration, the Kenyan government has never sought to redress fully the destruction and loss it instigated, nor has it addressed the political grievances that created the conditions for such violence. As a result, a significant number of people are still not back on their land today, and will probably never be. In some areas, the effect has been to reduce significantly the numbers of Kikuyu, Luhya, or Luo residents, in keeping with the calls by some high-ranking government officials for the expulsion of these ethnic groups from certain areas of the country. More importantly, the grievances that allowed for the manipulation and explosion of ethnic tension can as easily be fanned today as they were in the early 1990s.

As the Kenyan experience illustrates, UNDP is lacking expertise, capacity, and experience in certain areas critical to the success of programs for the internally displaced. Without taking further steps to improve its capacity, UNDP will be unable to fulfill the challenges presented by the expanded responsibilities that arise in situations with human rights and protection implications. The conclusions and recommendations of this report offer to UNDP suggestions of institutional steps that it can take to address the issues identified as impediments to reintegration. Such an examination is particularly valuable in light of UNDP's growing involvement in this area.

Human Rights Watch/Africa is calling on UNDP to ensure that human rights and protection components are a central part of its responsibilities in programs it administers for the internally displaced. Without doing so, its ability to successfully reintegrate the displaced, as evidenced from its own comparative experiences in Central America and Kenya, will not be as successful. Human Rights Watch/Africa believes that it is within UNDP's political mandate and capability to do better. UNDP needs to build on the encouraging efforts to interpret its mandate broadly and flexibly, and take the next step to ensure that its policy positions on governance, social justice, human rights, land tenure and protection are consistently and centrally translated into its program application. Human Rights Watch/Africa is calling on the U.N. Secretary-General to ensure that the basic principles of human rights protection are made integral to any U.N. operation aimed at internally displaced populations.

2. RECOMMENDATIONS

To the United Nations
To the Secretary-General and the U.N. Secretariat

- The U.N. needs to prioritize and improve coordination and cooperation between its humanitarian, development, human rights and peace-keeping agencies with regard to programs for the internally displaced. In designing such programs, it is critical that basic principles of human rights protection be made integral to any operation aimed at displaced populations.

- The U.N. Social and Economic Council is currently preparing recommendations to the secretary-general for improving U.N. coordination in humanitarian emergencies. The secretary-general should take steps to ensure that the recommendations are actively implemented by U.N. agencies.

- The representative of the U.N. secretary-general on internally displaced persons is currently preparing a body of principles, which will serve as a non-binding guide to governments and institutions. This body of principles recapitulates in one document the existing human rights obligations to the internally displaced, clarifies the gray areas, and remedies identifiable gaps. The secretary-general should require all U.N. agencies administering programs for the internally displaced to apply these principles in the field.

To the Representative of the U.N. Secretary-General on Internally Displaced Persons

- The representative of the U.N. secretary-general on internally displaced persons should undertake a mission to Kenya to raise awareness of and attention to the plight of the internally displaced, and work with the government and the U.N. to find solutions for those who remain displaced.

- The representative of the U.N. secretary-general on internally displaced persons should continue to work closely with UNDP, and other U.N. agencies, to suggest tangible ways that the body of principles being drafted by the representative can be incorporated into program implementation, particularly in the areas of human rights and protection.

To UNDP

- UNDP should formally recognize the necessity of changing its traditional working approach in some areas to order to address the full range of issues facing the internally displaced and to better implement such programs. In the same way that UNDP has innovatively defined its mandate to contribute in humanitarian emergency situations, it should take the next step and develop expertise in the areas of human rights and protection. UNDP needs to be willing to make institutional changes where necessary to deal with the issues that inevitably arise with programs for the internally displaced. UNDP should also be willing to coordinate and cooperate with other U.N. agencies that have the necessary expertise.

- The policies contained in UNDP's February 1997 submission to the ECOSOC review process for improving U.N. coordination in humanitarian emergencies should be widely circulated within UNDP. All staff members should be apprised of UNDP's mandate responsibilities to include human rights and protection concerns.

- In undertaking to coordinate emergency and development programs, UNDP needs be willing to advocate on behalf of internally displaced populations and, where necessary, challenge government abuses against the displaced. To better accomplish this protection role, UNDP should: (1) be willing to transform its traditionally close working relationship with governments in order to protect the displaced; and (2) address the inherent tensions that may arise when a resident representative, with a close working relationship with a government, is asked to serve as a resident coordinator on a program on the internally displaced which may require some criticism of government policy toward the displaced.

- UNDP resident representatives/resident coordinators and field staff should routinely receive training in international human rights and protection standards as well as advocacy strategies for the implementation of these standards. Relevant UNDP staff at headquarters should also be sensitized in these areas in order to ensure that they are giving the necessary support to UNDP staff in the field. This training could perhaps be jointly managed in cooperation with other agencies.

- UNDP should institute a data reporting procedure in its internally displaced programs as a routine matter to identify and register the displaced as well as to publicly document the cooperation of the government or controlling authority periodically. At a minimum, findings about the situation should be shared at frequent intervals with the emergency relief coordinator of the Department of Humanitarian Affairs, the representative of the secretary-general on internally displaced persons, and the high commissioner on human rights. Regular public reporting can deter human rights abuses by governments against the displaced, as well as ensure that human rights concerns are not subordinated to political considerations.

• A human rights unit should be created within UNDP which can serve as a focal point within the agency to ensure that its displaced persons programs are prepared to deal with the human rights issues which may arise. This unit should be involved in the conception of programs for the internally displaced from the outset. This unit should also be tasked with cooperating and liaising with the U.N.'s human rights agencies. Human rights concerns are central to finding solutions for the internally displaced. UNDP programs for the internally displaced should monitor and advocate for government compliance with human rights guarantees.

• UNDP should incorporate human rights and protection officers in all its programs for internally displaced populations, either from its own staff or seconded from other bodies, whose duty is to report on human rights issues, interface with the population and government or controlling bodies, and to take actions designed to prevent abuses and ensure accountability for violators.

• UNDP should as a routine practice establish a written agreement with the government, prior to the commencement of the program, which lays down minimum standards that must be complied with by those in power as a condition for international implementation of a program for the internally displaced. There should be no assistance without guarantees from the government or controlling authority that the U.N. mission will have free access to the displaced at all times, that the physical security and basic human rights of the displaced will be safeguarded, and that humanitarian assistance will be allowed to pass freely under U.N. control.

• It is widely agreed that UNDP's creation of a National Committee for Displaced Persons, which brought together representatives from the government, the donors, UNDP and the local and international NGO community, was a significantly positive contribution in Kenya. This approach should be retained by UNDP for future programs for the internally displaced.

- Where past human rights abuses are responsible for causing the internal displacement, UNDP should not operate its programs as if it is writing on a blank slate. Abuses of the past must be addressed for long-term resolution, and legal and administrative sanctions for perpetrators of human rights abuses should be a priority of any program for the internally displaced. Programs for the internally displaced should include a legal assistance component to help local NGOs and the displaced bring charges against the perpetrators of the violence. UNDP should be willing to press governments to bring charges against those responsible for the displacement, including high-ranking government officials.

- As a matter of priority, UNDP should cooperate and consult closely with local NGOs who are assisting the internally displaced. Displaced persons programs should include a component that builds the capacity of these local groups to assist and protect the displaced.

- Successes and failures of past UNDP programs should be examined and utilized by the agency to strengthen future programs. UNDP should set up an internal unit to review past programs, similar to the 'Lessons Learned' unit in the U.N.'s Department of Peace-Keeping Operations. The findings of this examination process must be actively incorporated into programs for the internally displaced through a systematic institutional procedure.

- UNDP should invite the representative of the U.N. secretary-general on internally displaced persons to work closely with UNDP to provide advice to UNDP to strengthen program implementation, particularly in the areas of human rights and protection.

- UNDP should take steps to assist those who remain displaced in Kenya. The Kenyan government has proposed in its most recent development plan, the Social Dimensions of Development Programme, that drought, cattle rustling and ethnic violence victims be treated as a single area of program focus. This approach may allow the government to further the myth that those displaced by the ethnic violence are just one more group affected by general poverty and crime, and allow the government to avoid its specific responsibility to voluntarily return those displaced by the ethnic clashes to their homes. UNDP should not participate in any assistance programs for those displaced by the clashes, without taking steps to monitor and ensure that the government does not use the opportunity to further its policies of removing certain ethnic groups from their land, particularly in the Rift Valley Province.

To Donor Governments and International Humanitarian Organizations

•   Donor governments and international humanitarian organizations should continue to follow the situation of the displaced in Kenya closely. Donor governments should continue to raise the issue of the internally displaced with the Kenyan government, to ensure that the government does not evade its responsibility to address past and continuing injustices against the displaced. Donors should call on the Kenyan government to respect the freedoms of movement, association, assembly and expression; to take steps to provide assistance and protection to reintegrate those who remain displaced; to hold accountable those responsible for the attacks; and to take steps to redress persistent reports of illegal land transfers, plot redemarcations, and land sales or exchanges being effected under duress.

•   Donors should support local NGO efforts to assist the internally displaced. In particular, legal assistance programs should be funded to assist the displaced to bring charges against those responsible for the violence and to challenge illegal or pressured land transfers.

•   Donor governments and humanitarian groups should not fund programs for those displaced by the ethnic clashes, unless steps are taken to ensure that the government does not use the opportunity to further its policies of removing certain ethnic groups from their land, particularly in the Rift Valley Province. The Kenyan government's proposal, in the Social Dimensions of Development Programme, that proposes to treat drought, cattle rustling and ethnic violence victims as a single area of program focus, could present such a danger. This approach may allow the government to further the myth that those displaced by the "ethnic" violence are just one more group affected by general poverty and crime, and allow it avoid its responsibility to voluntarily return all those displaced.

To the Kenyan Government

•   The government must take steps to address the plight of the tens of thousands who still remain displaced as a result of the ethnic clashes. Additional and adequate assistance, security, and protection must be provided for as long as it takes to enable the displaced to return voluntarily and permanently to their land. The government should concentrate on reintegration in areas where the displaced still cannot return to their land because of threats of renewed violence, especially in the Olenguruone-Molo, Enosupukia, Mt. Elgon and Burnt Forest areas.

•   The government must stop dispersing and harassing the internally displaced and those who assist the displaced. Displaced persons who were dispersed through threats or force by government authorities should be voluntarily returned to their place of former residence. Where legitimate reasons for relocation exist, adequate alternative sites should be provided with advance notice.

•   Police and KANU officials who have been responsible for brutality and harassment of the displaced, particularly at Maela camp in 1994, must be disciplined for their actions.

•   The Attorney-General's Office should set up an independent commission to inquire into the persistent reports of illegal land transfers, plot redemarcations, and land sales under duress. In cases where displaced victims have sold their land at below market prices because of the feared or actual insecurity caused by the "ethnic" clashes, the government should create a process through which such land transfers can be reviewed. Such transfers, may in fact, amount to constructive forced evictions. Victims should be entitled to return to their homes wherever possible, or to receive adequate compensation if not. This commission should also assist victims displaced as a result of the violence, where appropriate, by payment of compensation to those who have lost their land.

•   Continuing incidents and past attacks on ethnic grounds should be thoroughly investigated and charges brought where there is evidence against individuals alleged to be directly responsible for killings and destruction of property. In all cases, the criminal law must be applied without regard for ethnic group, political party, or other status. All allegations of the involvement of government officials in the violence should be investigated and charges brought where there is evidence sufficient to make a *prima facie* case of wrongdoing.

•   The government must take steps to address the periodic incidents of violence which continue to break out and ensure that government officials are not responsible for inciting "ethnic" violence in light of the upcoming national election due to be held before March 1998.

3. INTERNATIONAL LEGAL PROTECTIONS
FOR THE INTERNALLY DISPLACED

Worldwide, the number of people displaced within their own countries exceeds the number of those who have crossed international borders and become refugees.[3] Recent estimates set the internally displaced population at twenty million and the refugee population at fifteen million.[4] Often the internally displaced are fleeing the same persecution as refugees, the only difference being that refugees have crossed an international border. However, the result of this difference is a comparatively weaker response from the international community. Primary responsibility for the internally displaced rests with their governments, in compliance with international human rights and humanitarian obligations. Where governments are failing to provide adequate assistance and protection to internally displaced populations, the international community has a responsibility to hold such states accountable to their obligations under international human rights and humanitarian law. Yet despite growing internally displaced populations, the international community's response to this needy and vulnerable group remains varied and inadequate.

Symptomatic of the lack of international oversight is the fact that no internationally agreed-upon definition of the internally displaced exists at present. In 1992, a working definition was established by the U.N. Secretary-General as:

> ...persons who have been forced to flee their homes suddenly or unexpectedly in large numbers, as a result of armed conflicts, internal strife, systematic violations of human rights or natural or man-made disasters; and who are within the territory of their own country.[5]

---

[3] Article 1 of the 1951 Convention Relating to the Status of Refugees defines a refugee as a person who has a "well-founded fear of being persecuted for reasons of race, religion, nationality, membership of a particular social group or political opinion, is outside the country of his nationality and is unable, or owing to such fear, is unwilling to avail himself of the protection of that country."

[4] Amnesty International, *Respect My Rights: Refugees Speak Out*, (London: Amnesty International, March 1997), p.1.

[5] "Analytical Report of the Secretary-General on Internally Displaced Persons," U.N. Doc. E/CN.4/1992/23, February 14, 1992, para.17. The working definition is currently under review. This definition has been criticized for being both too broad and too narrow.

The same report found that natural disasters, armed conflict, communal violence and systematic violations of human rights are among the causes of massive involuntary migrations within state borders. Vulnerable and unable to find places of safety, internally displaced persons often suffer persistent violations of fundamental human rights, and their basic needs often go unmet.[6]

Despite the pressing nature of the problems facing the internally displaced, whose plight as uprooted people often does not differ much from refugees, there is no comparable treaty for protection of the internally displaced and no specific institution mandated to address their needs. While international refugee law can be used by analogy for standard-setting, it is not directly applicable to the internally displaced: the 1951 Convention Relating to the Status of Refugees and its 1967 Protocol which establishes the obligations of states towards refugees does not apply to persons within their own country.

There are numerous provisions within international law relevant to the rights of the internally displaced.[7] International human rights treaties apply to the internally displaced (as well as to all persons present in a country), including the International Covenant on Civil and Political Rights (ICCPR) and the International Covenant on Economic, Social and Cultural Rights (ICESCR). Specific treaties relating to the rights of women and children, to torture, and to racial discrimination may be relevant to particular protection concerns. Where internal displacement takes place against the backdrop of armed conflict, international humanitarian law also applies.

There are some objections to the inclusion of natural disasters in the text because those displaced in this manner would not qualify as refugees had they crossed the border. Others object to the wording "fleeing in large numbers" because this formulation excludes individuals fleeing individually or in small numbers. The wording "suddenly or unexpectedly" has also been questioned on the grounds that in some case internal displacement could be anticipated or take place over a long period of time. See Francis M. Deng, "Internally Displaced Persons: Report of the Secretary-General to the Fifty-First Session of the Commission on Human Rights," U.N. Doc. E/CN.4/1995/50, February 2, 1995, pp.32-35.

[6]"Analytical Report of the Secretary-General on Internally Displaced Persons," U.N. Doc. E/CN.4/1992/23, February 14, 1992, para.6.

[7]A comprehensive compilation of legal norms relevant to the internally displaced can be found in "Internally Displaced Persons: Report of the Representative of the Secretary-General, Mr. Francis M. Deng," submitted pursuant to Commission on Human Rights resolution 1995/57. U.N. Doc. E/CN.4/1996/52/Add.2, December 5, 1995.

In Kenya, the Moi government's actions towards the internally displaced has consistently been in violation of its international legal obligations. Under international law, governments must ensure that persons within their territory or jurisdiction are free from extra-legal or arbitrary killings, acts of violence and ill-treatment. According to articles 6 and 7 of the ICCPR, which Kenya has ratified, every human being is guaranteed the inherent right to life and to be free from torture and cruel, inhuman or degrading treatment or punishment. Governments also have a duty under Article 26 of the ICCPR to provide equal protection of the law. The U.N. Human Rights Committee, which monitors the compliance of all states parties with the ICCPR, has emphasized that the state not only has a duty to protect those in its borders from such violations, but also to investigate violations when they occur and to bring the perpetrators to justice.[8] A state may not choose to prosecute serious violations of physical integrity in a discriminatory fashion, protecting some individuals of certain ethnic groups and not others. Forced displacement by its nature gives rise to massive violations of the international right of the internally displaced to choose their own residence and to move freely within their own region and country. Freedom of residence and movement is guaranteed in article 12 (1) of the ICCPR.[9]

The guarantees of food, potable water, clothing and housing are also of great importance to those who have been internally displaced. Under international law, the Kenyan government is not allowed to discriminate in its fulfillment of its obligation to provide persons within its territory with the essentials needed for their survival. Yet, the government periodically destroyed or prevented relief supplies from reaching camps in areas where it knew this would affect certain ethnic groups, while not obstructing assistance to other areas. Under the ICESCR, which Kenya has ratified, the right to an adequate standard of living, including adequate food, clothing, and housing is recognized in article 11(1). Access to medical care is recognized by article 12. The Committee on Economic, Social and Cultural Rights has made clear in its general comments interpreting states' obligations under the treaty that states parties bear a "minimum core obligation to ensure the satisfaction of, at the very least, minimum essential levels of each of the rights." The committee has held that a state party "in which any significant number of

---

[8]Report of the Human Rights Committee, 37 U.N. GAOR Supp. (No.40) Annex V, general comment 7(16), para.1 (1982) U.N. Doc. A/37/40(1982).

[9]Derogation from this is permitted only to the extent necessary to "protect national security, public order, public health or morals or the rights and freedoms of others, and are consistent with the other rights recognized in the present Convention."

individuals is deprived of essential foodstuffs, of essential primary health care, of basic shelter and housing, or of the most basic forms of education, is *prima facie*, failing to discharge its obligations under the Covenant" unless it can "demonstrate that every effort has been made to use all resources that are at its disposition in an effort to satisfy, as a matter of priority, those minimum obligations."[10]

Primary responsibility for the rights of the internally displaced rests with their sovereign government, and any international assistance to an internally displaced population requires the acquiescence of the state. However, where governments are unwilling or unable to uphold their international legal obligations to promote and protect human rights, the international community is legally entitled, if not obliged, to become involved. International involvement usually occurs in such cases or when a government has invited an international presence to assist it with the problems of the internally displaced. In situations of armed conflict or civil strife, a government may be either unwilling or unable to fulfill its responsibilities, or in some cases, may itself be responsible for the displacement. In such cases, the need for international protection and assistance is all the more necessary.

> The Representative of the U.N. Secretary-General on Internally Displaced Persons, Francis M. Deng, appointed in 1992, has emphasized the profound physical and psychological trauma suffered by the internally displaced as a result of their displacement. On the run and often without documents, they have been more readily subjected to round-ups, forcible resettlement, and arbitrary detention. They are more vulnerable to forced conscription and sexual assaults, and more regularly deprived of food and health services. The highest mortality rates ever recorded during humanitarian emergencies have come from situations involving internally displaced persons.[11]

---

[10]General Comment of the Committee on Economic, Social and Cultural Rights, No.3, para.10. (Fifth session, 1990); General comments of the Committee on Economic, Social and Cultural Rights, Nos.1-4, reprinted in Note by the Secretariat, Compilation of General Comments and General Recommendations adopted by Human Rights Treaty Bodies, U.N. Doc. HRI/GEN/1/Rev.1 (July 29, 1994).

[11]Roberta Cohen, "Protecting the Internally Displaced," *World Refugee Survey 1996*, (U.S. Committee for Refugees, Washington D.C.: Immigration and Refugee Services of America, 1996), p.24. See also, Francis M. Deng, "Internally Displaced Persons: An

The inadequacies of the international system for providing protection and assistance to the internally displaced has become increasingly apparent as the numbers of internally displaced have escalated rapidly. In recent years, growing international concern has prompted the U.N. to begin to take steps to address the plight of the internally displaced. Since 1990, the U.N. has undertaken a number of initiatives to improve its capacity. Following a number of international conferences highlighting the plight of uprooted populations,[12] the General Assembly, at the recommendation of the secretary-general, determined in 1990 that UNDP resident coordinators based in the field could be assigned the function of coordinating assistance to internally displaced persons. The following year, the U.N. created the position of emergency relief coordinator in order to improve the U.N.'s response to emergency situations, including those involving displaced populations. Subsequently, the secretary-general created the Department of Humanitarian Affairs (DHA), to be headed by the emergency relief coordinator, to coordinate and facilitate timely and effective humanitarian responses at the U.N. secretariat.[13] That same year, with concerns over protection mounting, the U.N. Commission on Human Rights requested the secretary-general to prepare an analytical report on internally displaced populations, which was later presented at the 1992 U.N. Human Rights Commission meeting.[14]

Interim Report to the United Nations Secretary-General on Protection and Assistance," U.N. Department of Humanitarian Affairs and Refugee Policy Group, December 1994.

[12]The December 1988 Conference on the Plight of Refugees, Returnees and Displaced Persons in Southern Africa (SARRED); and the May 1989 International Conference on Central American Refugees (CIREFCA).

[13]See United Nations, *DHA in Profile*, (Geneva: United Nations Department of Humanitarian Affairs, July 1995), DHA/95/170; Roberta Cohen and Jacques Cuènod, *Improving Institutional Arrangements for the Internally Displaced*, (Washington D.C.: Brookings Institution—Refugee Policy Group Project on Internal Displacement, 1995); and Jacques Cuènod, "Coordinating United Nations Humanitarian Assistance: Some Suggestions for Improving DHA's Performance," (Washington D.C.: Refugee Policy Group, June 1993).

[14]Resolution 1991/25, March 5, 1991. This Resolution required the Secretary General to base his report on the information given by governments, specialized agencies and related organs of the U.N., regional and inter-governmental organizations, the International Committee of the Red Cross and nongovernmental organizations. The report, presented in 1992, was sub-titled "Alternative Approaches and Ways and Means within the United Nations System for Improving the Effective Enjoyment of Human Rights."

In order to focus further attention on the plight of internally displaced populations, two significant actions were taken in 1992. First was the appointment of a representative of the U.N. secretary-general on internally displaced persons, at the request of the U.N. Commission on Human Rights, to focus on the human rights dimensions of internal displacement and to study ways and means of promoting increased protection and assistance to internally displaced populations. Representative Francis Deng has been given the authority to discuss issues of internal displacement at senior governmental levels and to highlight the needs of internally displaced populations. Second, a Task Force on Internally Displaced Persons was established by the Inter-Agency Standing Committee (IASC). The IASC, which is composed of the heads of the U.N.'s major humanitarian and development agencies and several other organizations, is chaired by DHA and meets on an almost regular monthly basis.[15] In December 1994, on the Task Force's recommendation, the IASC designated the emergency relief coordinator of DHA to serve as the U.N's reference point for all requests for assistance and protection in actual or developing situations of internal displacement. The IASC also invited the representative on internally displaced persons and the high commissioner for human rights to participate in its work. Although the IASC's Task Force has reached agreement on crucial issues such as the appointment and responsibilities of humanitarian coordinators, it has much greater potential.

In August 1995, the fifty-four governments of the U.N. Economic and Social Council (ECOSOC) called for a review of the role, operational responsibilities, and capacities of the U.N.'s agencies in order to strengthen the coordination role in humanitarian emergencies. The ECOSOC resolution 1995/56 came in response to both the growing recognition that relief, rehabilitation and development activities must often occur simultaneously, and attention to this issue in the secretary-general's annual report calling for greater inter-agency coordination. The report argued that such a comprehensive review would

---

"Analytical Report of the Secretary-General on Internally Displaced Persons," U.N. Doc. E/CN.4/1992/23, February 14, 1992.

[15]Members of the IASC include the heads of DHA, the U.N. Children's Fund (UNICEF), UNHCR, World Food Program (WFP), the Food and Agriculture Organization of the U.N. (FAO), World Health Organization (WHO), UNDP, the International Organization of Migration (IOM), and the Red Cross Movement (the International Committee of the Red Cross (ICRC), the Red Crescent Societies, and the International Federation). The NGOs include the International Council of Voluntary Agencies and Inter-Action.

"facilitate efforts by Member States to address possible constraints, gaps and imbalances in the system which has evolved rapidly in an *ad hoc* manner in recent years."[16] The ECOSOC resolution asked the relevant U.N. agencies to report back on these issues and to consider a range of other issues including training, delegation of authority to the field, operational, financial and evaluation reporting; and the value of formal operational agreements between agencies. The resolution asked DHA to convene regular meetings with governments, U.N. agencies and other organizations to ensure that the matters raised in the ECOSOC resolution are coherently addressed. Completion of this major evaluation is expected by the end of 1997 and will hopefully lead to a simple and effective coordination structure at the field level as well as minimum operating standards in the areas of human rights and protection among others.

Additionally, the representative of the U.N. secretary-general on internally displaced persons is currently preparing a body of principles, which will serve as a non-binding guide to governments and institutions. This body of principles will recapitulate in one document the existing human rights obligations to the internally displaced, clarify the gray areas, and propose remedies for the identifiable gaps. These principles will not create a new legal status for the internally displaced, but rather will highlight the needs of the displaced and articulate specific legal solutions derived from the existing guarantees.

Despite these encouraging steps, the international response to emergencies involving the displaced remains *ad hoc*, limited, and in many cases, unsatisfactory.[17] Due to the widely differing situations and needs of internally displaced populations globally and the absence of a central U.N. agency tasked

---

[16]U.N. DHA, "Addressing the Gaps and Imbalances: The Challenge from ECOSOC," *Retrospective DHA 1995* (Geneva), March 1996, pp.6-7.

[17]See Francis M. Deng, *Protecting the Displaced: A Challenge for the International Community* (Washington D.C.: Brookings Institution, 1993); International Committee of the Red Cross, *Internally Displaced Persons Symposium, Geneva, October 23-25, 1995* (Geneva: International Committee of the Red Cross, 1996); Roberta Cohen and Jacques Cuènod, *Improving Institutional Arrangements for the Internally Displaced,* (Washington D.C.: Brookings Institution—Refugee Policy Group Project on Internal Displacement, 1995); Roberta Cohen, "Protecting the Internally Displaced," *World Refugee Survey 1996,* (U.S. Committee for Refugees, Washington D.C.: Immigration and Refugee Services of America, 1996), pp.20-27; and Stephanie T.E. Kleine-Ahlbrandt, *The Protection Gap in the International Protection of Internally Displaced Persons: The Case of Rwanda,* (Geneva: Université de Genève Insititut Universitaire de Haute Etudes Internationales, July 1996).

with protection of internally displaced, a variety of U.N. agencies have been involved in providing programs for the displaced. The level of assistance varies from country to country, making for an uneven international response. There is an ongoing debate as to whether strengthened implementation of the existing human rights norms, despite their shortcomings, is the best approach or whether changes to the international legal normative framework that specifically deal with the internally displaced should be made. In either case, more needs to be done to protect the rights of the internally displaced, and the challenge to the international community is to find a way to respond to and address the unique needs of this group in the most effective manner.

4. UNDP'S MANDATE TO ADDRESS
HUMAN RIGHTS AND PROTECTION ISSUES

Every U.N. agency has a responsibility to promote and protect human rights. According to the Preamble of the U.N. Charter, the U.N. was formed to:

> reaffirm faith in fundamental human rights, in the dignity and worth of the human person, in the equal rights of men and women...; [and] to establish conditions under which justice and respect for the obligations arising from treaties and other sources of international law can be maintained; and to promote social progress and better standards of life in larger freedom.

Although some U.N. agencies have expressly designated human rights mandates and possess specialized technical expertise in the area of human rights, this does not diminish the responsibility of all agencies to incorporate human rights concerns into their work. Article 1(3) of the U.N. Charter includes a mission for all U.N. agencies to "promot[e] and encourag[e] respect for human rights and for fundamental freedoms for all without distinction as to race, sex, language, or religion." As Secretary-General Kofi Annan confirmed shortly after taking office, human rights constitute a part of development work.[18]

UNDP has a broadly defined mandate to promote sustainable human development. Its work has traditionally been concentrated outside of conflict or emergency situations, partnering itself closely with governments, to administer or fund development programs. It has never interpreted its role as formally including human rights work, either in a monitoring and reporting capacity or to include active measures to those in its charge. Within the context of the growing number of major humanitarian emergencies, all U.N. agencies are being challenged to tailor their work to address the growing numbers of internal conflicts and the massive refugee and internally displaced flows. Like other U.N. agencies, UNDP is grappling to stretch its traditional capacity in order to address the operational challenges posed by the exigencies of forced displacement. This section does not provide a comprehensive critique of UNDP's mandate. It is meant to draw attention to certain developments and statements by UNDP that are directly relevant to its administration of programs for the internally displaced.

---

[18]"U.N. Reform: The First Six Weeks," Statement by Kofi Annan, U.N. Secretary-General, New York, February 13, 1997.

While situations of internal displacement can differ widely, the one common feature that all share is the central role that human rights plays. Human rights abuses usually accompany the violence and displacement, and human rights protection issues are inevitably integral to the success of reconciliation and reintegration efforts. Protection entails both physical security as well as defending the legal and human rights of the displaced. Human rights abuses during the course of a reintegration program can undermine and eventually stall international efforts. If U.N. agencies administering reintegration programs for the internally displaced marginalize or exclude human rights concerns, they will not succeed in their mission.

UNDP has taken up the challenge of interpreting its mandate more innovatively to respond to emergency situations, including internal displacement.[19]

---

[19]UNDP's eight programmatic categories for intervention in crisis situations are:

(1) Emergency Interventions: a. Resources for disaster assessments; b. Crisis management and support for relief delivery; c. Support for program initiatives.

(2) Programming for Peace and Recovery: a. Participation in consolidated inter-agency appeals; b. Organization of special consultations or round tables; c. Ad hoc programing missions; d. Monitoring of aid flows; e. Establishment of early warning systems; f. National long-term perspectives; g. Development mapping of districts and regions.

(3) Area Rehabilitation to Resettle Uprooted Populations: a. Resettlement and reintegration of displaced persons; b. Restoration of health and education services; c. Rebuilding infrastructure and production systems; d. Local planning and participatory mechanisms; e. Environmental rehabilitation.

(4) Reintegrating Demobilized Soldiers: a. Operational support during cantonment; b. Organization of severance pay and other aid packages; c. Matching job and training opportunities with demand; d. Organization of credit schemes for self-employment.

(5) Demining: a. Operational and institutional support; b. Mine prevalence surveys and data base.

(6) Rebuilding Institutions and Improving Governance: a. Analysis of civil service reform needs; b. Coordination of capacity-building programs; c. Decentralization and local government; d. Observance of human rights; e. Land reform and regulation of land tenure.

(7) Organizing National Elections: a. Training in election procedures and logistics; b. Voter registration and supervision of polling; c. Organization of observer presence.

Gradually, UNDP is expanding its traditional interpretation of its mandate to include work in crisis situations where it can "bridge relief with development."[20] Being mandated to deal with "the entire development process,"[21] it seeks to contribute in conflict or crisis situations where emergency relief and development

---

(8) Managing Delivery of Program Aid: a. Monitoring and supervision of commodity aid; b. Procurement of imports.

UNDP Emergency Response Division, *Building Bridges Between Relief and Development: A Compendium of the UNDP Record in Crisis Countries* (New York: undated).

[20]According to UNDP, "[t]his does not mean that the UNDP role is all-encompassing; rather it means that it can provide an overview and fill gaps as part of fulfilling its development mandate...In emergency humanitarian response, UNDP has no primary role, only a supportive one, helping to harmonize development with relief. However, in rehabilitation and recovery, UNDP plays a lead role, working together with others...Whatever the specific type of intervention, the principles of development responses to emergencies are the same: curative development programmes and assistance to Governments and communities with[*sic*] re-building their capacities are essential if humanitarian assistance is to contribute to lasting solutions. In countries with humanitarian emergencies, development interventions must continue wherever they can and interrupted development activities must quickly be resumed so that governments and communities can sustain livelihoods and detach themselves from external relief as early as possible." "Further Elaboration on Follow-up to Economic and Social Council Resolution 1995/56: Strengthening of the Coordination of Emergency Humanitarian Assistance," U.N. Doc. DP/1997/CRP.10, February 28, 1997, para.37.

[21]UNDP Emergency Response Division, *Building Bridges Between Relief and Development: A Compendium of the UNDP Record in Crisis Countries* (New York: undated), p.3, 6. See also, "Further Elaboration on Follow-up to Economic and Social Council Resolution 1995/56: Strengthening of the Coordination of Emergency Humanitarian Assistance," U.N. Doc. DP/1997/CRP.10, February 28, 1997, paras.2, 3, which states: "While saving lives has priority over sustaining livelihoods, and while emergency relief is not part of the UNDP mandate, there is a growing understanding that development does not cease during emergencies. If relief efforts are to contribute to lasting solutions, sustainable human development (SHD) must continue to be vigorously supported, complementing emergency action with new curative initiatives that can help to prevent a relapse into crisis. While emergencies call for innovative responses from UNDP, the Programme must remain dedicated to the promotion of development in such contexts. Particular groups or geographical areas should sometimes be targeted by both relief and development organizations together, placing a premium on team work. The 'bridging of relief with development' requires close coordination with those leading emergency activities."

opportunities overlap. In this regard, it views programs for the internally displaced as a primary example of where it can contribute and envisions growing involvement in this area.

UNDP's role was formally expanded in 1989 by the U.N. secretary-general to permit UNDP resident representatives based in the field, to be designated as U.N. resident coordinators in order to be the focal point for coordinating relief to internally displaced populations.[22] The following year, a General Assembly resolution assigned to U.N. resident coordinators "...the function of coordinating assistance to the internally displaced, in close cooperation with Governments, local representatives of donor countries and the United Nations agencies in the field."[23] UNDP's eight programmatic categories for emergency-type programs include "Area Rehabilitation to Resettle Uprooted Populations" which includes programs for the "resettlement and reintegration of displaced people." With regard to the internally displaced, UNDP has adopted a broad interpretation of its role as:

(a)   supporting development of the communities that the displaced have rejoined; and

(b)   facilitating joint planning of different interventions well beforehand, to ensure that development activities are synchronized with relief. Quick post-return projects are followed by more complex action of continuing development and growing government and community involvement. Since the fundamental socio-economic unit of reintegration is the household, attention to the specific needs of women is important.[24]

According to UNDP, its programs for the internally displaced are "designed to revitalize commercial networks, foster local participation in decision-

---

[22]Report of the Secretary-General, U.N. Doc. A/44/520, September 28, 1989, p.19; and Statement by Abdulrahim A. Farah, Under-Secretary-General for Special Political Questions, before the Third Committee of the General Assembly, November 14, 1989.

[23]General Assembly Resolution 44/136, February 27, 1990.

[24]"Further Elaboration on Follow-up to Economic and Social Council Resolution 1995/56: Strengthening of the Coordination of Emergency Humanitarian Assistance," U.N. Doc. DP/1997/CRP.10, February 28, 1997, para.14.

making, to restore social cohesion and link rehabilitation with development change."[25] Another relevant category of UNDP's emergency work to the internally displaced is that of "Rebuilding Institutions and Improving Governance," which includes, among other things, the "coordination of capacity-building programmes; observance of human rights; and land reform and regulation of land tenure."[26]

UNDP has recognized that human rights, governance, social justice and land reform are all important issues, within the ambit of its mandate, deserving of attention and critical to the successful implementation of emergency-type programs. In response to the 1995 ECOSOC review of the capacity of the U.N. system in humanitarian assistance, UNDP articulated the evolving interpretation of its mandate in a February 1997 document.[27] In clarifying its role toward the internally displaced, UNDP's vision of what factors are important to include in a program are strikingly similar to those that Human Rights Watch/Africa has identified in this report.

UNDP formally acknowledges, in its February 1997 document, that its programs for the internally displaced must incorporate the issues of governance, social justice, human rights, land tenure and protection. UNDP maintains that measures to strengthen various aspects of the capacity for governance are particularly important because "[s]uccessful recovery implies broad development challenges, meeting needs for adequate legal frameworks, judiciaries, police systems, stable social and political environments, and sufficient economic opportunities."[28] It believes that "[s]ocial justice in general must be addressed in efforts to foster reconciliation,"[29] and that "[j]ustice and human rights is another

---

[25]UNDP Emergency Response Division, *Building Bridges Between Relief and Development: A Compendium of the UNDP Record in Crisis Countries* (New York: undated), p.12.

[26]Ibid., p.4.

[27]"Further Elaboration on Follow-up to Economic and Social Council Resolution 1995/56: Strengthening of the Coordination of Emergency Humanitarian Assistance," U.N. Doc. DP/1997/CRP.10, February 28, 1997.

[28]Ibid., para. 6.

[29]Ibid., para. 36.

important area with a critical development component."[30]   In the area of land reform and the regulation of land tenure, it recognizes that "within a limited framework, such as area rehabilitation schemes, considerable progress can be made with project assistance in securing titles for peasants."[31]

Increasingly, there is also a recognition that protection responsibilities must be a part of programs for the internally displaced. As part of the ongoing ECOSOC review, recommendations have been put forward jointly by the relevant agencies through the Inter-Agency Standing Committee (IASC) (whose membership includes UNDP Administrator Gustave Speth). The April-May 1997 recommendations of the IASC to the U.N. secretary-general's office recommend that UNDP resident representative/resident coordinators continue to assume responsibility for internally displaced programs where appropriate.   The recommendations go further, stating that the responsibilities of the resident representative/resident coordinator will include: "serving as an advocate for the assistance and protection of IDPs [internally displaced persons]."[32]

It is unfortunate that many of these responsibilities which UNDP has recognized as being within its mandate as well as critical to the success of programs for the internally displaced were not applied in the Kenyan program. In reading this report, which deals with a program administered between 1993 and 1995, it is important to recognize that some of UNDP's current positions had not been articulated as clearly at that time. Frederick Lyons, UNDP resident representative to Kenya pointed out:

> Remember that in 1993, the U.N. mandate on the internally displaced was still being hammered out. When David Whaley [former UNDP resident representative to Kenya] took over this project, it was a new area for the U.N. For UNDP specifically, it was an evolution of our thinking about development issues and what that constituted in our work. The project in Kenya should be seen as an early experience, warts and all, as being a half successful attempt to stabilize conditions and to raise the key

---

[30]Ibid., para. 35.

[31]UNDP Emergency Response Division, *Building Bridges Between Relief and Development: A Compendium of the UNDP Record in Crisis Countries* (New York: undated), p.22.

[32]IASC recommendations, DHA, April-May 1997 (unpublished).

issues and risks. It was an early attempt for UNDP to find practical solutions to problems of this nature.[33]

UNDP deserves credit for its progress at the policy level to interpret its mandate progressively and more comprehensively since that time. However, UNDP appears somewhat ambivalent about its recognition that human rights are central to the success of its emergency programs. While acknowledging that human rights is an "important area with a critical development component,"[34] UNDP has balked at translating this unequivocal recognition of the importance of human rights into tangible program objectives within the agency. Calling it a "pragmatic" approach, UNDP has shied away from making a strong commitment, preferring to see its contribution as complementing other U.N. bodies, such as the Centre for Human Rights. UNDP also appears to be deterred by the prospect that in raising human rights issues it may encounter resistance from abusive or uncooperative governments.

> ...In the observance of human rights, which constitutes a critical factor for social peace and political legitimacy, UNDP is adopting a pragmatic strategy of approaching these issues in geographically limited settings. Human rights is a matter of such central importance to society that tackling it head-on at the national level, even where clear legislation has been enacted, often creates serious problems.[35]

Moreover, the progressive positions articulated in the ECOSOC document do not yet appear to be the only definitive interpretation that UNDP puts forward on human rights. The response provided to Human Rights Watch/Africa in April 1997 to the draft of this report contained a disturbing position which appeared to

---

[33]Human Rights Watch/Africa interview, Frederick Lyons, UNDP Resident Representative to Kenya, Nairobi, August 22, 1996.

[34]"Further Elaboration on Follow-up to Economic and Social Council Resolution 1995/56: Strengthening of the Coordination of Emergency Humanitarian Assistance," U.N. Doc. DP/1997/CRP.10, February 28, 1997, para. 35.

[35]UNDP Emergency Response Division, *Building Bridges Between Relief and Development: A Compendium of the UNDP Record in Crisis Countries* (New York: undated), p.22.

contradict the above-stated policy positions, as well as Secretary-General Kofi Annan's February 1997 comment that human rights is a part of development work. UNDP, in its explanation of why the Kenyan program did not address human rights concerns, put forth the position that human rights is a "sovereign" issue which it has no mandate to deal with. UNDP stated:

> At no time did ...UNDP imply that it had the capacity or mandate to become the primary advocate against human rights violations in Kenya. Much of the criticism contained in the HRW [Human Rights Watch] report is basically a misinformed commentary on UNDP's 'failure' to be the international human rights monitor, arbitrator and advocate in Kenya during the crisis. This indicates HRW's misunderstanding of UNDP's role and its limitations to engaging in 'sovereign' issues for which it has no mandate. Instead of blaming UNDP for not solving the human rights problems in Kenya, the report should identify the link between human rights violations and the policy of the Government at that time.[36]

Human Rights Watch/Africa is not calling on UNDP to be the primary advocate for all human rights violations taking place in Kenya or any other country. Human Rights Watch/Africa does, and has in this report, identified the links between human rights violations and the Kenyan government. However, that does not relieve UNDP of its obligations under the U.N. Charter—in programs that it is administering—to ensure that human rights and protection concerns are fully incorporated.

---

[36]See Appendix: "UNDP Response to Human Rights Watch Report," UNDP, New York, April 1997 [hereafter Appendix: UNDP Response], p.7.

5. KENYA'S INTERNALLY DISPLACED: STATE-SPONSORED ETHNIC VIOLENCE [37]

In late 1991, concerted domestic and international pressure for political liberalization and respect for human rights forced the government of President Daniel arap Moi to legalize a multiparty system. In August 1991, an internal democracy movement had demanded an end to the monopoly on power held by KANU, which had led Kenya since independence in 1963. President Moi, however, claimed that the return to multiparty rule would threaten the stability of the state by polarizing the country along ethnic lines. By the time multiparty elections were held at the end of 1992, it appeared that his claim was accurate: Kenya's political parties had divided largely along ethnic lines, and "tribal clashes" in the rural areas of western Kenya had left hundreds dead and tens of thousands displaced. The great majority of the victims came from the ethnic groups associated with the political opposition. By 1993, Human Rights Watch/Africa estimated that 1,500 people had died in the clashes and that some 300,000 were displaced. The clashes pitted Moi's small Kalenjin tribe and the Maasai[38] against

---

[37]Much of the information in this section was published previously in Human Rights Watch/Africa, *Divide and Rule: State Sponsored Ethnic Violence in Kenya* (New York: Human Rights Watch, November 1993); Human Rights Watch/Africa, "Multipartyism Betrayed in Kenya: Continuing Rural Violence and Restrictions on Freedom of Speech and Assembly," *A Human Rights Watch Short Report*, vol. 6, no. 5, July 1994; Human Rights Watch, *Playing the "Communal Card:" Communal Violence and Human Rights* (New York: Human Rights Watch, April 1995), pp.97-112; and Human Rights Watch/Africa, "Kenya: Old Habits Die Hard: Rights Abuses Follow Renewed Foreign Aid Commitments," *A Human Rights Watch Short Report*, vol. 7 no. 6, July 1995.

[38]The Kalenjin, which make up about 11 percent of the Kenyan population, consist of a number of smaller groups speaking Nilotic languages and sharing similar cultural traditions. In precolonial times, the Kalenjin were largely pastoralist and the various subgroups had few political links; the sense of common "Kalenjin" identity was born as a result of British colonial policies and has strengthened since independence. President Moi is a Kalenjin. The Maasai are Nilotic-speaking pastoralists who originally grazed their animals over a wide area and were later restricted to a reserve along the border with Tanganyika (Tanzania). The division between "pastoralist" and "cultivator" is, however, a generalization: most groups practiced a mixed agriculture.

the populous Kikuyu, Luhya, and Luo tribes.[39] For a while, Kenya, previously an example of relative stability in the region, teetered on the brink of a low-level civil war.

The Moi government capitalized on unaddressed land ownership and tenure issues, dating back to the colonial period. During colonial rule, pastoral ethnic groups on the land in the Rift Valley area were ousted to provide land to British settlers. Following independence in 1963, much of this same land was used to settle squatter laborers who had been previously used as cheap agricultural labor on the settler farms.

After independence, Kenya became a de facto one-party state led by KANU, following the voluntary dissolution of the Kenya African Democratic Union (KADU)[40] which had advocated ethnic regionalism and another party, the African People's Party.   KANU rule under president Jomo Kenyatta was characterized by strong Kikuyu nationalist sentiments. Moreover, the land issue was never fully addressed. British settler interests were safeguarded, while no effort was made to deal with the competing claims of those pastoral ethnic groups who originally were ousted from the Rift Valley area by the British and the squatter laborers who subsequently settled on the land. Consequently, large tracts of some of the best farmland in Kenya remain owned by British settlers. For those settlers

---

[39]The Kikuyu, one of the largest ethnic groups in Kenya, make up about 21 percent of the population. The Kikuyu are of a Bantu-language group, and were the group most immediately and drastically impacted by colonization, both by the alienation of their land and also in gaining the most rapid access to education and thus political influence. The Luo, which make up approximately 13 percent of the population, speak a Nilotic language closer to the languages of the Kalenjin than that of the Kikuyu and live mostly in the region abutting Lake Victoria. The Luhya, who generally live in the west of Kenya, make up approximately 14 percent of the population and also consist of a number of smaller groups that were grouped together during the colonial period.

[40]The Kenya African Democratic Union (KADU), of which future President Moi was a leader, was a party of ethnic minorities, such as the Kalenjin and Maasai, who claimed original use of the British settler land. KADU pursued a political philosophy of regionalism, majimboism in Kiswahili, which would allow semi-autonomous regions, based on ethnicity, to have substantial decision-making power. The central government, in turn, would have a limited and defined federal role. Majimboism was seen as the only political option to safeguard the rights of the minority groups. Believing that its interests would be better served by supporting KADU, the British settler population was quick to provide KADU with financial support to counter KANU. Eventually KANU won a pre-independence election with a decisive majority resulting in a compromise to protect British settler interests.

who wanted to sell their land, land settlement schemes were set up with the newly independent government to assist the former squatter labor to buy land either individually or through collective schemes.

Among the Kikuyu, unlike communal pastoral groups, such as the Maasai and Kalenjin, farming was an established practice. Accordingly, many Kikuyus were eager to take advantage of the opportunity to purchase land. Encouraged and assisted by President Kenyatta, a Kikuyu, large number of Kikuyus bought land in the Rift Valley in the 1960s and 1970s and moved from the overcrowded Central Province. These farms were at the center of the "ethnic" violence of the 1990s. The instigators drew on the competing land claims in order to inflame violence among certain ethnic groups.

When Kenyatta died in 1978, Vice-President Moi succeeded him as president. As Kenyatta had used political power to give disproportionate benefits to his own Kikuyu ethnic group, so Moi did for the minority Kalenjin. Kalenjin and members of allied groups such as the Maasai were appointed to key positions within the local and national government administration. In 1982, to forestall the registration of a new party by politicians discontented with the increasing severity of his rule, the constitution was amended to make Kenya a de jure one-party state. An abortive coup attempt several months later was followed by a crackdown on all potential opponents.

By 1990, repression had provoked a vigorous movement in support of a multiparty system. In August 1991, an opposition coalition calling itself the Forum for the Restoration of Democracy (FORD) was formed to demand multipartyism. At least partly in response to these demands, the consultative group of bilateral donors to Kenya suspended more than U.S.$1 billion of balance of payments support and other aid in November 1991 on economic, governance, and human rights grounds. One month later, in December 1991, article 2(a) of the Kenyan constitution, outlawing opposition parties, was repealed.

As the campaign for multiparty democracy gained strength and then developed into a full election campaign, violence broke out between different ethnic groups, particularly in the Rift Valley, Western and Nyanza provinces, the heart of the "white highlands" during colonial times. The "tribal clashes," as they became known, first broke out in October 1991 on the border of the three provinces, and rapidly spread to neighboring districts. By December 1991, when parliament repealed the section of the constitution making Kenya a one-party state, large areas of western Kenya had been affected as tens of thousands were displaced from their land.

Eyewitness reports of the attacks were remarkably similar. Bands of armed "Kalenjin warriors" attacked farms belonging to the Luo, Luhya, and

Kikuyu, the groups from which FORD drew its main support, destroying homes and driving the occupants away or killing those who resisted. The attackers were often dressed in an informal uniform of red or black t-shirts, their faces marked with clay in the manner of initiation candidates, and armed with traditional bows and arrows or pangas (machetes). The attacks by the Kalenjin warriors had in almost all cases been carried out by organized groups. Local Kalenjin often reported that outsiders had come to tell them that they had to fight and that the Kikuyu or others were planning to attack them. They also reported that they were promised the land of those they attacked. By contrast, where counter attacks had been mounted by Kikuyu, Luhya, or Luo, they were usually more disorganized in character, and by no means as effective in driving people away from their land. The great majority of those displaced were members of the Kikuyu, Luhya, and Luo ethnic groups.

Although it seemed that the first outbreak of fighting was a simple land dispute between members of the Luo and Kalenjin groups, the violence rapidly took on the content and ethnic breakdown of the wider political debate. FORD, the leader of the call for multipartyism, was dominated by Kikuyu, Luo and, to a lesser extent, Luhya, at both leadership and grassroots levels. Although the coalition included members of other ethnic groups and based its political platform on the misuse of power by President Moi, it built much of its appeal on the resentment of its supporters to the domination of the government by Moi's own ethnic group, the Kalenjin, and its allies, the Maasai. Moi, for his part, portrayed the calls for multipartyism as an anti-Kalenjin movement and played on the fears of the minority ethnicities at the return to power of the economically dominant Kikuyu. At the same time, he argued that Kenya's multiethnic nature meant that multiparty politics would inevitably break down on ethnic lines leading to violence.

Kalenjin and Maasai politicians opportunistically revived the idea of majimboism, ethnic regionalism, championed by KADU at independence. KANU politicians close to Moi revived the calls for majimboism as a way of countering the demand for multipartyism in Kenya. Under the cover of a call for regional autonomy, prominent politicians demanded the forcible expulsion of all ethnic groups from the Rift Valley, except for those pastoral groups—Kalenjins, Maasai, Turkana and Samburu—that were on the land before colonialism. A number of majimbo rallies were held calling for "outsiders" in the Rift Valley to return to their "motherland,"[41] or for "true" Rift Valley residents to defend themselves from

---

[41]Republic of Kenya, *Report of the Parliamentary Select Committee to Investigate the Ethnic Clashes in Western and other parts of Kenya*, (Nairobi: Government Printer, September 1992), pp.8-9.

opposition plots to eliminate the indigenous peoples of the valley. While many Kenyans have no quarrel with the concept of regionalism, *per se*, they viewed these calls as nothing less than ethnic expulsions.

Although the rise of the violence was clearly linked to the emergence of multipartyism and drew on longstanding tensions between Kenya's different ethnic groups, evidence rapidly emerged that the clashes of late 1991 and after, far from being the spontaneous reaction to competition among parties divided along ethnic lines, were deliberately provoked by elements within the government. Soon after the clashes first erupted, rumors of the involvement of government ministers and officials began to circulate. More systematic investigations followed. In April 1992, the National Council of Churches of Kenya (NCCK), the coalition of Protestant churches that was heavily involved in providing relief to the victims, issued a report that linked high-ranking government officials. It concluded: "These clashes were and are politically motivated...to achieve through violence what was not achieved in the political platform, i.e. forcing majimboism on the Kenyan people."[42] A further report issued by a coalition of groups in June 1992 stated that the attacks were organized under central command, often in the presence of local administration and security officers and that warriors who were arrested were often released unconditionally.[43]

Mounting pressure from opposition and church groups eventually forced President Moi to authorize an official investigation. In September 1992, the parliamentary select committee appointed for this task delivered a sharply critical report confirming many of the earlier allegations, with all the more force because the committee, since it was formed before the elections, was made up only of KANU members. The report concluded that the attacks had been orchestrated by Kalenjin and Maasai politicians close to the president, including the vice-president and some members of parliament. The Kiliku report, as it came to be known after committee chair, cited evidence that the "Kalenjin warriors" carrying out the attacks had been paid by these officials for each person killed or house burnt down, and that government vehicles had transported the warriors to and from clash areas. The report recommended that "appropriate action be taken against those administration officials who directly or indirectly participated or encouraged the

---

[42]*The Cursed Arrow: Organized Violence Against Democracy in Kenya* (Nairobi: NCCK, April 1992), p.1.

[43]*Interparties Symposium I Task Force Report*, Nairobi, June 11, 1992.

clashes."[44] The report was not adopted by the full KANU parliament, and no effort was made by the government to implement its recommendations.

During 1992, the bloodshed escalated rapidly, as the opposition mobilized for the election. The clashes decreased in intensity somewhat toward the end of the year, when international attention focused on the country during the lead-up to the elections which were finally held on December 29, 1992. KANU was returned to power.[45] The KANU victory was based on only 36 percent of the popular vote and owed much to the government's manipulation of the electoral process and to the division—largely on ethnic lines —of FORD into two parties, FORD-Kenya and FORD-Asili, to which was added a breakaway group from KANU, the Democratic Party (D.P.).[46]

Many expected that the clashes would cease after Moi's election victory. Although some areas were restored to calm, periodic outbreaks of violence continued throughout 1993 and 1994. In some areas, residents who returned to their farms after being driven off were attacked a second or even third time. In April 1993, a further report was published by a group originally set up to monitor the elections, that confirmed previous conclusions of government instigation and complicity and documented attacks that took place following the election.[47] Hopes that the attacks would end and that the displaced would be permitted to go home were raised yet again with the announcement of the joint Kenyan

---

[44]*Report of the Parliamentary Select Committee to Investigate Ethnic Clashes in Western and Other Parts of Kenya* (Republic of Kenya: Government Printer, September 1992), p.82.

[45]Although there were widespread allegations of irregularities in the conduct of the poll, international observers concluded that "[d]espite the fact that the whole electoral process cannot be given an unqualified rating as free and fair...we believe that the results in many instances directly reflect, however imperfectly, the will of the people." *The Presidential, Parliamentary and Civic Elections in Kenya: The Report of the Commonwealth Observer Group* (London: Commonwealth Secretariat, 1993), p.40.

[46]FORD-K remained relatively multiethnic, but was dominated by Luos, Luhyas, and members of some smaller groups. Later in 1993, further fault lines developed within the party between the Luo and other leaders. FORD-Asili and DP were both seen as Kikuyu parties, divided along regional lines.

[47]*Courting Disaster: A Report on the Continuing Terror, Violence and Destruction in the Rift Valley, Nyanza and Western Provinces of Kenya* (Nairobi: National Election Monitoring Unit (NEMU), April 29, 1993).

government/UNDP program in late 1993. However, in 1994, violent clashes broke out again in the Burnt Forest and Molo areas respectively. In 1994, the victims of the violence were increasingly Kikuyu.

Those whose lives were shattered by the killing and destruction fled to relatives, church compounds, nearby abandoned buildings, makeshift camps, and market centers. Often, the shelters where the displaced have congregated for years at a time have been overcrowded, unsanitary, and inadequate. Many were forced to create open makeshift structures of cardboard and plastic sheeting and to sleep outdoors. Food was often cooked under filthy conditions and many of the displaced routinely suffered health problems, such as malaria, diarrhoea and pneumonia. These conditions worsened during the rainy season. Frequently, local government officials would downplay the magnitude of insecurity in their area and disperse victims without providing adequate assistance or security to permit them to return to their land, putting them at risk.

Children, who constituted an estimated 75 percent of the displaced, were deeply affected. Many children had witnessed the death of close family members, and in some cases, had suffered injuries themselves. As a result, reports of children displaying aggressive behavior or suffering nightmares were common. The education of children was disrupted, in many cases permanently. Where parents and volunteers attempted to create makeshift schools at camps, local government authorities were known to close down the schools, depriving the children of any formal educational opportunity whatsoever.[48]

A study of the situation of displaced women in one camp in Kenya found that women had suffered rape and other forms of sexual assault during the clashes. After becoming displaced, the study found that gender inequalities were exacerbated. Displaced women were victims of "rape; wife-beating by their husbands; sexually-transmitted diseases; poverty; manipulation; hunger, fear, anger, anxiety; trauma, despondency, dehumanization; heavy workload and physical fatigue."[49] The report also noted that the women shouldered a bigger

---

[48]Human Rights Watch/Africa, *Divide and Rule*, pp.80-83.

[49]Naomi W. Gathirwa and Christine Mpaka, "Reproductive and Psycho-Social Needs of Displaced Women in Kenya," the U.N. Development Fund for Women (UNIFEM) and UNICEF, *Reproductive and Mental Health Issues of Women and Girls Under Situations of War and Conflict in Africa: Proceedings of an Expert Group Consultation*, (Nairobi: Regal Press, November 1994), p.49. See also, Dr. Naomi Gathirwa, "Report on the Psycho-social Needs of the Displaced Women in Maella and Thessalia Camps: Field Visit by the FIDA Team from July 25-30, 1994," Nairobi, August 1994; and Human Rights

burden: they often risked returning to farm on their land because the men feared death if they returned; they frequently ate less in order to feed their husbands and children first; and they often suffered miscarriages or complications in childbirth due to the lack of an adequate diet and the harsh living conditions.

Although there are those who assert that this ugly chapter in Kenya's history is over and that the government has abandoned its policies of ethnic persecution, they forget the thousands of victims who still remain displaced and dispossessed. If the Moi government has retreated from the use of large-scale ethnic attacks, it is because this tactic is no longer politically expedient or necessary. The government's policies of ethnic persecution and violence have served it well: The government conceded to an international presence and was forced to retreat from a full-scale expulsion of select ethnic groups from the Rift Valley Province. But, on the whole, it did not divert much from its intentions, and in large part succeeded in doing what it set out to do when it instigated the violence in 1991.

Watch/Women's Rights Project, *The Human Rights Watch Global Report on Women's Human Rights*, (New York: Human Rights Watch, August 1995), pp.100-140.

6. THE UNDP/KENYAN GOVERNMENT
DISPLACED PERSONS PROGRAM: 1993-1995

The Kenya Program

Following pressure from international donors about the ethnic violence in Kenya, the government agreed in 1993 to cooperate with the U.N. to initiate a program to return the internally displaced to their homes. In May 1993, a U.N. Disaster Management Team traveled freely through the Rift Valley Province and met with a wide range of people, including the displaced, the local administration and NGOs and church groups.[50] The U.N. team concluded that conditions were far worse and the numbers of persons displaced far greater than the government acknowledged and recommended to the government that urgent action was needed. The report noted that the displaced population had been living in:

> appalling conditions for up to one and a half years, with irregular supplies of food; no adequate shelter; no access to schooling for the children and only occasional access to basic health facilities...people who had trusted in the Government's assurances that security had been reestablished had returned home to face sudden death at the hands of their former neighbors.[51]

The mission also enabled the U.N. team to assess the needs of the population. Those needs were found to be not so much for short-term humanitarian relief, but

---

[50]In March-April 1993, a U.N. Disaster Management Team received reports of continued suffering among populations displaced through ethnic clashes in the Rift Valley despite the denial by the government of any significant problem. The U.N. team decided to consider whether the experience previously acquired through a drought alleviation program could be applied to the search for solutions to the ethnic violence in the Rift Valley. According to UNDP, the U.N. team hoped to build on the good-will, methodology, and team work that had developed with the local administrations, NGOs, community groups and donors through the drought program. The delegation consisted of David Whaley, UNDP; Vicent O'Reilly, UNICEF; Else Larsen, WFP; Steve Oti, WHO; G. Guebre-Christos, UNHCR; Don Ferguson and Robert Palmer, U.N. Volunteers assigned to the Emergency Relief Unit through DHA operating under the responsibility of the U.N. Disaster Management Team. See Appendix: UNDP Response, p.1.

[51]U.N. Disaster Management Team, *Mission to the Affected Areas of Western Kenya Affected by the Ethnic Clashes*, May 1993, p.1-2.

rather those aspects of the situation which the NGOs and churches providing assistance to the displaced felt they could not handle alone. The main problems revolved around security, registration, land-tenure problems, and long-term development goals. According to UNDP:

> the U.N. team agreed that these problems could not be solved by the population alone, supported by the NGOs and church communities, but required the participation of the local and national administration. Without a commitment by the government to ensure safety, to clearly condemn ethnic violence, to tackle the underlying causes of the conflict and to foster long-term development there could be no prospect of return for the majority of the displaced persons nor lasting solutions to the crises that had occurred in 1992. These conclusions were shared by the persons consulted on the ground including the Roman Catholic Bishop of Nakuru and Eldoret, who urged the U.N. team to involve the government in the search for solutions, stressing that the U.N. was better placed to raise this issue than others.[52]

The team concluded that there was a need for the U.N. to play a positive role in addressing this "ongoing national emergency" by sending technical teams to develop strategies and programs. The report rightly cautioned that such efforts had to be accompanied by a government commitment at the highest levels to create the conditions conducive to reconciliation, reintegration and enhanced security.[53] Following a meeting with the president, to present the findings of the report, the government agreed to the creation of a program along the lines that had been recommended.

The selection of UNDP as the implementing agency for the Kenya program in 1993 was indicative of the trend towards broadening UNDP's traditional development mandate to encompass more emergency-type situations with national development implications. Such a role utilizes UNDP's well-established expertise in development-oriented issues, while requiring it to develop

---

[52]See Appendix: UNDP Response, p.1-2.

[53]Ibid.

additional capacities, particularly in the relief assistance, human rights and protection areas.[54]

In October 1993, UNDP and the Kenyan government announced a joint "Programme for Displaced Persons," which proposed a $20 million plan for reconciliation and resettlement.[55] The commencement of the UNDP/ Kenyan government program coincided with concerns expressed by Kenya's donors about the ethnic violence. At a Consultative Group meeting on aid to Kenya held in Paris on November 22 and 23, 1993, the chairman's closing statement mentioned that "bilateral donors were disturbed by the ethnic clashes [and]...underlined the paramount importance of strengthened Government action to defuse the underlying tensions and deal with unrest through evenhanded application of the law."

The UNDP program in Kenya was intended to reintegrate the people who had been displaced by the "ethnic" violence since 1991, estimated by UNDP at the time of the report at about 255,000 (and by 1994, at 260,000): with children accounting for as much as 75 percent of that population and female-headed households comprising an estimated 40 percent.[56] The stated objective of the program was "the reintegration of displaced populations into local communities, prevention of renewed tensions and promotion of the process of reconciliation."[57]

The Rogge Reports

Specific proposals for action were developed in a report written by UNDP consultant John Rogge known as the "Rogge Report" (the first of two).[58] On the

---

[54]Other UNDP involvement with the reintegration of internally displaced populations has occurred in Cambodia, Central America, Mozambique and the Horn of Africa.

[55]Government of Kenya/UNDP, *Programme Document: Programme for Displaced Persons*, Inter-Agency Joint Programming, October 26, 1993.

[56]John Rogge, "The Internally Displaced Population in Nyanza, Western and Rift Valley Province: A Needs Assessment and a Program Proposal for Rehabilitation," UNDP, September 1993, part 3(3.8).

[57]"Programme for Displaced Persons and Communities Affected by the Ethnic Violence," UNDP, February 1994.

[58]John Rogge, "The Internally Displaced Population in Nyanza, Western and Rift Valley Province: A Needs Assessment and a Program Proposal for Rehabilitation," UNDP, September 1993 [hereafter Rogge Report I, UNDP, September 1993].

basis of this report, the UNDP/Government of Kenya program was developed and approved by the government towards the end of the year. The 1993 Rogge report provided a well-written synopsis of the situation. It identified three basic groups of displaced. First, were those who had returned and were in the process of rehabilitating their homes and farms. Second, were those who were commuting to their farms to cultivate, but were not able or willing to return because of the perception or experience of continued insecurity. Third, were those who would probably never be able to return to the land they were driven off, either because the remaining residents were emphatic about never allowing any other ethnic group to reclaim their land or because they were squatters with no legal claim to return. In some areas, this land was left abandoned, uncultivated and unoccupied. In others, farms were illegally occupied by remaining residents either for cultivation or grazing livestock.

More importantly, the Rogge report correctly identified both the short-term and long-term needs for successful reintegration. In the immediate short-term, the report called for food, shelter and agricultural materials to be provided as well as the establishment of a revolving credit scheme to provide capital for cash crop farming or small scale business. In the medium-term, it recommended that more general development initiatives needed to be undertaken that benefitted entire communities regardless of status, including rehabilitation of destroyed institutions such as schools and health centers, while linking these initiatives to efforts such as reconciliation seminars, skills and employment training, and regularization of the land tenure system. For long-term reintegration, the report underscored that protection and security issues were paramount for the success of the program as was the need to address development issues, most notably land registration and tenure security. In cases where return to one's land was unlikely to materialize, lasting alternative arrangements were called for. The report noted that "no single partner has the capacity to single-handedly deal with the complex issues being faced,"[59] and called for a partnership of UNDP, the government and the local NGOs/churches. An overall duration of two years for short-term activities was envisioned and a five-year program for medium-term activities.[60]

The program, on the basis of the Rogge report, soon got under way under the auspices of UNDP's Nairobi-based Project Implementation Unit. The program focused on the worst hit areas in three provinces: Western Province (Bungoma and Mt. Elgon Districts); Nyanza Province (Kisumu District); and the Rift Valley

---

[59]Ibid., Executive Summary, para.14.

[60]Ibid.

Province (Elgeyo-Maraquet, Nakuru, Nandi, Trans Nzoia and Uasin Gishu Districts).[61] Program assistance was administered through the funding of quick impact activities, known as "quips," which are rapid, low budget interventions targeted at the most urgent needs identified by the communities. These small grants are usually aimed at the transition phase from emergency relief into rehabilitation. The Rogge report identified key areas where program support for quips was needed including relief, agriculture and shelter assistance; income generating activities; capacity building for local institutions; programs to support women and women-headed households; rehabilitation of economic and social infrastructure; and strengthening of civil and land registration.[62] UNDP noted:

> Besides the immediate relief element, projects will be supported which are developmental, promote self-reliance and are ultimately locally sustainable. Quips will be limited in time (three to six months) and by the ceiling of funds available per project...Quips can be submitted by communities, committees, NGOs, churches, and also government departments; they should be the result of dialogue based on well defined needs expressed by the communities themselves who should be actively involved at all stages.[63]

A year later, in August 1994, John Rogge returned to Kenya to examine the work in progress: to assess its effectiveness, to identify residual needs for relief and rehabilitation, to identify mechanisms to tackle the root causes of the clashes, and to establish sustainable development activities.[64] He had a five-week contract

---

[61]Government of Kenya/UNDP, *Programme Document: Programme for Displaced Persons*, Inter-Agency Joint Programming, October 26, 1993, p.18.

[62]Rogge Report I, UNDP, September, p.29.

[63]UNDP, "Programme for Displaced Persons and Communities Affected by Ethnic Violence," Nairobi, February 1994, p.6.

[64]John Rogge, "From Relief to Rehabilitation, Reconstruction and Reconciliation: Developments and Prospects for Internally Displaced Populations in Western and Rift Valley Provinces," UNDP, September 1994 [hereafter Rogge Report II, UNDP, September 1994]; and presentation by David Whaley, former UNDP Resident Representative to Kenya, contained in the minutes of the third Excom meeting, Kenyatta International Conference Centre, Nairobi, September 8, 1994.

during which time he revisited the clash-affected areas.[65] The report's assessment of the situation was upbeat about prospects for return and the government's commitment to the process. The 1994 report concluded that major incidents of violence had decreased and security had continued to improve. On the whole, the report found that cultivation had revived in the clash areas. This improvement was credited to a turnaround within the government. The report stated:

> Although the majimbo debate continues to be actively promoted by certain figures, there has nevertheless been a pronounced and increased effort at all levels of government to reduce tensions and address the question of finding durable solutions to the problems of the displaced and other clash-affected persons. It is therefore disappointing that a few key figures continue to deflect attention from progress that is being made. At most district and divisional administration levels, there have been complete changes in personnel over the past year, and the administrative officers were seen to be committed to the resolution of conflict in their areas. Cooperation between local administration and the Displaced Persons Program (DPP) is very encouraging.[66]

The report also acknowledged that in some places the situation was still variable and that threats and harassment continued. The report listed some eight areas where people were still not able to return to their homes, including in Uasin Gishu District (the Kipkaren valley and parts of Turbo and Burnt Forest); parts of South Nandi district; Trans Nzoia district (the eastern slopes of Mt. Elgon); Nakuru district (Olenguruone division and Maela camp); and Kericho district (Thessalia mission).

Although the second Rogge report refrained from publishing many statistics, the report estimated that about one-third of the affected population had returned, and that in western Kenya a much larger proportion (close to half) were

---

[65]UNDP states that Mr. Rogge spent well over three weeks in the clash areas. See Appendix: UNDP Response, p.2. The minutes of the third Excom meeting, Kenyatta International Conference Centre, Nairobi, September 8, 1994, cite Mr. Rogge as saying he spent twelve days in the field.

[66]Rogge Report II, UNDP, September 1994, Executive Summary, para.2.

in a critical stage of transition.[67] In some areas, the return was complete, and in others, people still commuted to their land in the day and slept at market centers at night. The report noted that a greater proportion of displaced Kalenjins appeared to have returned. The main reasons cited for not returning were insecurity or fear of violence, lack of materials to rebuild destroyed homes, and dependency on relief distributions.[68] The report estimated that of the displaced, some 20 percent would probably never be able to return to their land without "circumspect and realistic political intervention."[69]

The major recommendation of the 1994 Rogge report in no uncertain terms was that UNDP needed to move away from short-term relief assistance and "quip" projects, and move toward meeting the medium and long-term needs of the displaced. Noting that UNDP had been concentrating on food distributions and agricultural inputs, the report identified the need for sustainable projects such as credit schemes for small businesses and agricultural extension services, and employment and job training programs.   For long-term reintegration and reconciliation prospects, the Rogge report stressed that UNDP had to tackle the problems associated with land tenure. The report read:

> A completely unresolved question, and which is clearly one [of] the major contributing factors to the clashes, is that of land tenure and the issue of obtaining title to land. Delays in surveying, failure to provide land titles, irregularities in the district land titles offices, misappropriation of funds and misallocation of plots by administrations of cooperative land holding societies, and an array of other ambiguities caused by sub-divisions of plots, non-formal (traditional) sales and/or exchanges of land, have together produced widespread uncertainty and contradiction over land ownership and rights to use land. This situation has been flagrantly exploited by the forces which incited the clashes. While the problems of land tenure irregularities and land titles acquisition are clearly a

---

[67]Ibid. para.4 and 5.

[68]Ibid.; and presentation by John Rogge, UNDP consultant, contained in minutes of the third Excom meeting, Kenyatta International Conference Centre, Nairobi, September 8, 1994.

[69]Rogge Report II, UNDP, September 1994, Executive Summary, para 6.

responsibility of the GOK [Government of Kenya], unless the specific problems and ambiguities in clash-areas are adequately addressed, the risk of renewed conflict remains. The DPP's [Displaced Persons Program] role in this regard must be to monitor ongoing problems and ambiguities and attempt to bring together the respective protagonists with local administrations.[70]

The Rogge report concluded with optimistic anticipation that with adequate donor funding:

there is no reason why the DPP [Displaced Persons Program] could not achieve its objectives within two years and be in a position to wind-up its operation. The critical assumption that must be made in this scenario is that there will be no further ethnic violence and that the GOK [Government of Kenya] intensifies its commitment to addressing and eradicating the root causes of the violence.[71]

---

[70]Ibid., para.21.

[71]Ibid., para.25.

7. GOVERNMENT UNDERMINING OF THE UNDP PROGRAM [72]

*"The despair of the displaced and refugee populations is an
abuse to human dignity and reasoning."*
      —*President Daniel arap Moi, Jamhuri Day speech, December
1996* [3]

The optimistic assessment of the reintegration process contained in the
second Rogge report, was not without cause. Some reintegration did occur in 1994,
particularly in Nyanza and Western Provinces, and there was a gradual return to
normalcy. Violence had reduced greatly over what existed a year earlier and many
people were in varying stages of return. In relation to the preceding two years,
these were significant improvements relative to the highly-charged and volatile
situation that had existed. While there was good reason to be heartened by these
improvements, however, serious obstacles to full reintegration remained.

The 1994 Rogge report's oblique references to individuals in government
who were continuing to incite violence and undermine reintegration understated the
extent to which the government remained an unwilling partner. At no time was the
Moi government ever a genuine partner in the UNDP endeavor. Through a dual
process of active obstruction on some fronts and complete inaction on others, the
government managed to undermine the UNDP program throughout. Alongside the
reintegration which was occurring in some areas, there was a pattern of
intimidation and a callous disregard for the displaced among government officials
both at the local and national level.

The decline of the large-scale attacks, the return of the displaced in some
areas, and the personal initiative of a small number of local administration officials
to cooperate with the UNDP program appear to have been interpreted by UNDP as
signaling an end to the government's policies of ethnic persecution and a
commitment to the UNDP program. UNDP states:

the fact that violence surged in a few areas because of a small
group of powerful, manipulative politicians cannot be put at the
doorstep of UNDP or the U.N. system. It is ingenuous [for

---

[72]This chapter uses some information previously published in Human Rights
Watch/Africa, *Divide and Rule* and Human Rights Watch/Africa, "Multipartyism Betrayed."

[73]Kenyan Ministry of Foreign Affairs and International Cooperations, "Kenya
Update," no. 5, December 21, 1996, p.1.

Human Rights Watch/Africa] to suggest that the U.N. programme's optimistic attitude in early 1994 was inappropriate because the government reverted to its former policy which contributed to an escalation of violence in late 1995 [*sic*][UNDP must mean late 1994. By late 1995 the program had ended].[74]

Human Rights Watch/Africa recognizes that ultimate responsibility lies with the Kenyan government, and that UNDP does not bear responsibility for the actions of the government. However, UNDP bears responsibility for not being a vigorous advocate on behalf of the rights of the displaced where government actions undermined the objectives of its reintegration program. Human Rights Watch/Africa does not find UNDP's response inappropriate because later events proved otherwise. Rather, the sections of this report that follow indicate that during 1994 itself, reintegration, while underway, was being limited and undermined on a regular basis by government actions.

UNDP's public characterization of local officials as being largely "committed to the program," and its diminutive portrayal of government abuse as being the setbacks of a "few key figures," was not wholly accurate and left the distinct impression that the government was by and large cooperating. The 1994 Rogge report mitigated both government and UNDP responsibility to act, while undermining the efforts of other agencies and NGOs to bring international pressure on the government to reverse and remedy its abusive policies. While UNDP had reason to be pleased with the gradual progress being made, the climate of mistrust and perceived insecurity which persisted in many parts of the Rift Valley should have been cause to place this progress within the context of the significant difficulties which remained and to recommend steps that could have been taken by UNDP at that time. Ultimately, the government was able to systematically undermine the UNDP program through inadequate security; uneven and discriminatory application of the legal system; harassment of the displaced, relief workers and journalists; illegal land transfers; and forced dispersals.

While it is true that the government abandoned its high-visibility tactics of terror and violence which had attracted national and international protest, it only did so after it had succeeded in displacing a significant number of people of certain ethnic groups from select areas. After achieving this end, all it had to do was to drag its feet to prevent a complete and permanent reintegration. Certainly, with the level of international and national scrutiny surrounding the displaced, the government had to give the appearance of supporting reintegration efforts, and

---

[74]Appendix: UNDP Response, p.3.

even allow some to return to their land. Among the first to return to their land, once material assistance was provided, were many of the Kalenjin farmers who had been displaced in retaliatory attacks. However, in fundamental ways, the Kenyan government never committed itself to the reintegration of the displaced, not during the UNDP program and not now.

Inadequate Security or Protection

The lack of adequate security and protection was a consistent theme both during the violence and the reintegration process with regard to physical security of person and property, security for the returning displaced to live on their land and harvest crops without fear, and security of land title or lease. On all counts, the government has failed to provide these guarantees comprehensively.

During the height of the violence, eyewitnesses consistently alleged that members of the security forces had failed to take any action against the attackers. In some cases, police who were present at the scene of an attack had refused to respond to appeals for help, simply standing by and watching people being driven out of their houses. In others, police based at nearby posts would only arrive to assist clash victims well after attackers had left, despite earlier calls for action. This prior history with the security forces left the displaced with a well-founded and deep-rooted distrust of the government. Throughout the reintegration process, continuing incidents, threats and fears of renewed violence prevented many of the displaced from returning to their land. Little was done by the government to conduct confidence-building measures that would have sent a clear message to the nation that the government was not prepared to countenance the ongoing security threats to reintegration.

In September 1993, after two years of inaction in providing additional security, and soon after the highly publicized visits of representatives of two foreign human rights organizations to the clash areas, the government declared three "security operation zones" giving the police emergency-type powers, excluding "outsiders," preventing the publication of any information concerning the area when deemed necessary, and banning the carrying of weapons in the worst-affected areas of the Rift Valley Province.[75] For most of the duration of the UNDP program, the restrictions were in force. They were lifted in March 1995.

---

[75]The Preservation of Public Security (Molo, Burnt Forest and Londiani areas) regulations, 1993. Kenya Gazette supplement Number 60, September 17, 1993. Under the constitution, the president has the power to seal off any part of the country when public order is threatened. These powers are also set out in Part III of the Preservation of Public Security Act.

However, even when they were in place, the extra security precautions in these zones did not prevent a large outbreak of "ethnic" violence in the Burnt Forest area in March 1994, which left at least eighteen dead and perhaps 25,000 displaced.

Burnt Forest was an area that was particularly hard hit and, for some, this was the second or even third time they had been displaced. Communities in Burnt Forest were first attacked in December 1992 and then in January, February, April and August 1993 and January 1994. The attacks in Burnt Forest in March 1994, which continued for a week, left the disturbing impression that the government was unable or unwilling to take effective measures to stop the clashes. In the meantime, the government was using the security legislation to restrict access to the area to journalists, NGOs and, on occasion, even to UNDP staff. In comparison to past incidents, the outbreak of violence in a security operation zone resulted in a prompter response from the local administration and security forces, although some residents accused the government of having had a hand in instigating the violence. The government also provided a small amount of food aid which was received by the displaced, whereas in the past, food relief pledged by the government was often never actually received by the displaced.[76] But as a journalist who writes on ethnic conflict in Africa noted, no one ever questioned how armed attacks on such a large scale could have broken out in an area under emergency regulations, particularly since sporadic incidents since January should have indicated that it was imminent:

> The Kenyan journalists were really exasperated at UNDP's willingness to be an apologist for the Kenyan government. Here you had a situation where there were emergency security powers in place and David Whaley [former UNDP Resident Representative to Kenya] was holding a press conference to say how amazing it was that the government had managed to get the violence under control so quickly. The surprise was that the violence had even happened in a security zone.[77]

In a March 1994 pastoral letter, the nation's Catholic bishops criticized the government's inaction on preventing the ethnic violence in the security operation zones:

---

[76]Human Rights Watch/Africa, "Multipartyism Betrayed," pp.3-15.

[77]Human Rights Watch/Africa interview with Bill Berkeley, journalist, New York, February 11, 1997.

The government has not spared any efforts to persuade public opinion that the clashes are caused by the opposition leaders, but Kenyans now have the conviction that these clashes could not have taken place nor continued for such a long time without the passive and sometimes active collaboration of the authorities. Should Kenyans believe that our numerous, well trained and well equipped army and police can be defeated by a small group of village warriors armed with pangas and rungus? Should we believe that the police and the army did their best but unfortunately always arrived late?[78]

At a press conference held in Nairobi on March 28, thirteen displaced Kikuyu residents of Burnt Forest issued a statement complaining that the local authorities had not taken any action even against known perpetrators of the violence. The displaced stated:

We want to tell the world that these clashes are occurring in the so-called security zones which the government brought into force last year. We want to remind the world that the government blamed earlier clashes on outsiders. Hence the idea of security zones to keep outsiders out...The current wave of arson, murder and destruction of property is aimed largely at the Kikuyu in the area...[but] all administrative positions in the area are held by Kalenjins to whom we cannot report when we are killed or our property is stolen or destroyed. We have been attacked a thousand times in the presence of the D.C. [District Commissioner], D.O. [District Officer], chiefs and assistance chiefs and their policemen and yet nothing is done. The policemen merely fire in the area. Warriors walk openly with arrows and bows and are never arrested...our children are sick with sleeping in the cold. Our families are hungry. We want the

---

[78]"On the Road to Democracy," pastoral letter issued by the Kenya Episcopal Conference, March 12, 1994, as reported in *Economic Review* (Nairobi), March 21-27, 1994, p.9.

world to intervene on our behalf. The aim of these crimes is to drive Kikuyus out of Burnt Forest.[79]

Other attacks on a smaller scale occurred sporadically elsewhere in the country throughout the duration of the UNDP program. For example, in January 1994, approximately 4,000 Kikuyus fled from their homes at Mwoyoi Scheme and Nyandonche, Ibere, Nyaiguta, Masimba and Tilango farms in Trans-Mara sub-district of Narok province, after their farms had been attacked by Maasais. The Kikuyu owners alleged that a meeting had been held at Lolgorien division headquarters of the local administration, which non-Maasais had been barred from attending, where a resolution had been passed to evict them. On February 21, there was a raid by approximately fifty Kalenjins on Kianjogu village at Laikipia district. The attack resulted in several injuries and the death of one Kikuyu, Kuria Njoroge, as well as the burning of houses. The victims of the attack reported that their attackers identified themselves as "tribal executioners who will return soon to finish all of you."[80] On May 1, 1994, eight were killed and twenty-six seriously injured when over one hundred attackers chanting majimbo slogans attacked Mtondia village, approximately ten kilometers from Kilifi town in Coast province, hundreds of miles from the Rift Valley, where the clashes had previously centered. The houses and property of predominantly Luo residents were destroyed and looted. Approximately 2,000 people fled the area following the attack. The attack had been preceded by the circulation of anonymous leaflets stating "if you are a Luo, the road to Kisumu is wide open, we have no mercy, we shall fight you." Journalists who attempted to visit the area after the attack were prevented by police who had sealed off the area.[81]

The sporadic incidents of violence and the occasional large outbreaks did nothing to engender confidence among the displaced. The then UNDP resident representative to Kenya, David Whaley, had stated that a necessary precondition for the success of the reintegration program was that the government create "an

---

[79]Press statement by farmers from the Burnt Forest security zone of Uasin Gishu district of the Rift Valley Province, Nairobi, March 28, 1994.

[80]"Evicted Group in Plea," *Daily Nation* (Nairobi), February 19, 1994.

[81]"Thousands Flee in Fear of Fresh Attack," *Daily Nation* (Nairobi), May 4, 1994 and "Luos Targeted in Violence, Kilifi Attack: A Genesis of Clashes at Coast?" *Clashes Update* (Nairobi: NCCK), no.16, May 25, 1994.

enabling environment."[82] It is fair to say that the government never created an enabling environment on a national scale. There was no effort by the government to mobilize its security forces effectively to prevent violence, to take preventive measures to avert threats of violence or to put forward government representatives from all the affected ethnic groups to promote solutions to the ethnic violence in cooperation with UNDP. Among the local government authorities, the ethnic mix is in no way proportionally representative of the populations in the area. Local government positions at the Provincial Commissioner (P.C.), District Commissioner (D.C.), District Officer (D.O.), chief and sub-chief levels are heavily dominated by Kalenjin appointees. The government has also relied on other ethnic minority groups with no ties to the displaced, such as Somali-Kenyans, in the clash areas to promote their policies. Throughout the UNDP program, the Kenyan government assigned only trusted Kalenjins from the Office of the President as national program coordinators to oversee the UNDP initiative.   When the government perceived that the first national program coordinator, Zakayo Cheruiyot, was becoming too cooperative with UNDP, he was replaced by the even more loyal Paul Langat, who had been notorious for his lack of concern toward the displaced when he served as D.C. for Uasin Gishu district.[83]

In most cases where Kalenjins were driven off their land in retaliatory attacks, they were generally able to return to their land once they were provided with material assistance to rebuild their destroyed homes. However, in many of the hardest hit areas, particularly around Eldoret and Nakuru in the Rift Valley Province and on the slopes of Mt. Elgon in Western Province, where these factors are absent, the government's inaction is evidenced by the thousands of predominantly Kikuyu, Luhya, and Luo displaced who remain off their land to date. In interviews with Human Rights Watch/Africa in August 1996, the most frequently cited reason for not returning to their land was the fear of renewed violence and a lack of confidence that government authorities would provide any

---

[82]"Enabling Environment a Must to Resettle Victims," *Clashes Update* (Nairobi: NCCK), vol. 2, no. 11, December 18, 1993.

[83]Human Rights Watch/Africa telephone interview with former UNDP Displaced Persons Program official (name and location withheld by request), March 12, 1997. This remains the case to date. In June 1996, the UNDP Resident Representative to Kenya Frederick Lyons was accompanied on a national visit to the ethnic clash areas by cabinet member Kipkalia Kones, a Kalenjin whose past record has included threats to multiparty supporters and incitement to ethnic violence (see section on Uneven and Discriminatory Application of the Law).

protection to the displaced if it did break out. A displaced Kikuyu man from Olenguruone in the Rift Valley Province told Human Rights Watch/Africa that they would willingly return to their land if they could, but the security risk was too high:

> Life has been hard since the clashes. How does one feed the family with no land? For one year we were on food from the Catholic church after our farms at Korofa were attacked by a group of people with spears, pangas and arrows in April 1992. Since 1993, I have been working as a casual laborer. When people around this area try to return to their land, some are killed. In 1992, someone was killed when they went back. I cannot risk going back until I am certain there is enough security.[84]

A thirty-five-year-old Luhya women from Western Province, who was widowed as a result of the violence, said:

> I was chased off my land in Kimama in 1992 with my five children when the attackers came. My husband was killed. I have tried to go back to my farm. The first time I went back in September 1994, I rebuilt the roof and doors, which had been stolen from the house, and began to plant maize. But I was chased off my land again by a group of Kalenjins who came with clubs to threaten me. One of them even had a gun. They fired in the air, and I ran away. I have been living in Namwele since then because I fear to return. I rent a place here, and I go back to farm my land in the day time. But I do not dare return. The roof and door that I had replaced were taken down. Sometimes I find some of my maize and beans uprooted and left there. These are signs to me not to return. If something happens, there is no one that I can get help from. My husband is dead, and the police will not help me.[85]

---

[84]Human Rights Watch/Africa interview with displaced man (Kikuyu), Elburgon, Nakuru district, Rift Valley Province, August 7, 1996.

[85]Human Rights Watch/Africa interview with displaced woman (Luhya), Namwele, Bungoma district, Western Province, August 3, 1996.

A much smaller number cited the lack of building materials for rebuilding their destroyed homes as the reason for their continued displacement, particularly in Western Province. Some have decided that they do not dare to chance returning to their land until after the next national election to be held by March 1998, because of the possibility of renewed violence and a complete lack of confidence in the government.

Uneven and Discriminatory Application of the Law

An important impediment to full reintegration, which was completely ignored by UNDP, has been the impunity enjoyed by the organizers of the violence and the attackers. The lack of accountability directly undermines reconciliation and long-term reintegration efforts in several ways. First, a critical factor in reconciliation and peace work is the importance of ensuring that justice is done. The ability of communities to put behind them the injustices they have suffered at the hands of another community is furthered if there is a sense that justice was done in acknowledging the wrongs committed against them. Second, holding those responsible for their actions—particularly in ethnic conflict—recognizes that certain individuals within a group were responsible for such acts, mitigating the blanket condemnation against the whole ethnic group, which otherwise inevitably arises and creates a lingering suspicion and hatred against the group generally. Third, because many of those accused of masterminding the clashes were high-ranking government officials, investigation and condemnation of their role in furthering the violence would have sent a strong message that the government would no longer tolerate the blatant misuse of power by its officials.

Yet, there has been a general failure by the government, during the UNDP program and since, to investigate reports of the involvement or collusion of government officials in the attacks, at all levels of responsibility. President Moi has consistently denied even the possibility that members of his government might be involved in instigating the clashes, alleging instead that members of the opposition, journalists, church leaders and "certain foreign embassies" were stirring up tribal hatreds. Claiming from the outset that the clashes were the consequence of ethnic rivalries stirred up by multipartyism, he has repeated these claims to date despite all evidence to the contrary.

The findings of the government's own parliamentary select committee's report which concluded that the violence had been orchestrated by Kalenjin and Maasai "individuals" close to the president have never been further investigated. The parliamentary report provides evidence that high-ranking politicians, including Vice-President George Saitoti and Members of Parliament Ezekiel Barngetuny,

Nicholas Biwott, Rueben Chesire and Wilson Leitich, funded and aided the "warriors," that government vehicles and helicopters had transported the "warriors," and that the local administration and security forces did not react to the situation with the required urgency. The report's recommendation that "appropriate action be taken against those administration officials who directly or indirectly participated [in] or encouraged the clashes" has never been acted upon.[86]

High-ranking Kalenjins and Maasai within the government have freely called for the expulsion of non-pastoralist groups who settled in the Rift Valley Province after independence.[87] The presence of the UNDP program neither deterred messages of ethnic hatred from being sent to communities by certain government officials nor prompted the government to punish such speech in cases where it constituted an incitement to violence.[88] In November 1993, Kalenjin Member of Parliament Nicholas Biwott called for majimboism at a rally in Kericho district, warning other ethnic groups that they would only be welcome in the Rift Valley if they respected the rights of the original inhabitants (Kalenjins, Maasais, Samburu and Turkana).[89] Kipkalia Kones in the Office of the President attended

---

[86]Republic of Kenya, *Report of the Parliamentary Select Committee to Investigate Ethnic Clashes in Western and Other Parts of Kenya* (Nairobi: National Assembly, September 1992).

[87]High-ranking government officials who were responsible for holding and attending rallies that called for action to be taken to expel "outsiders" from the Rift Valley Province and to "crush" multiparty advocates, include Nicholas Biwott, George Saitoti, William ole Ntimama, Kipkalia Kones, Joseph Misoi, Henry Kosgey, John Cheruiyot, Timothy Mibei, Eric Bomett, Willy Kamuren, Paul Chepkok, Benjamin Kositany, Ezekiel Barngetuny, Francis Medway, William Kikwai, John Terrer, Lawi Kiplagat, Christopher Lomada, Peter Nagole, Ayub Chepkwony, Robert Kipkorir and Samson ole Tuya.

[88]In its response, UNDP says "[Human Rights Watch/Africa] refers to the UNDP Programme not 'deterring messages of hatred,' however odious, from being disseminated. How could it?"

UNDP misunderstands Human Rights Watch/Africa here. We are only noting that government officials continued to feel embolded to make such statements of ethnic hatred even in the face of the UNDP program which the government was a partner to. This was indicative of a problem. We were not blaming UNDP for failing to end these statements. Appendix: UNDP Response, p.3.

[89]"'Majimbo' is the Answer—Biwott," *Daily Nation* (Nairobi), November 29, 1993.

majimbo rallies at which he declared that the Rift Valley Province would only have Kalenjin Members of Parliament and made statements to the effect that anyone who supported the opposition would "live to regret it."[90] In April 1994, KANU Assistant Minister Shariff Nassir told Kenyans that until Kenya reverted to a one-party state, the ethnic violence would continue. Home Affairs Minister Francis Lotodo gave a speech on November 28, 1993, telling Kikuyus that they had forty-eight hours to leave West Pokot district. He also warned that the Kalenjin community would take the law into its own hands if they did not comply with this order. Following his threat, local administration officials reiterated the message.[91]

In other cases, where these pronouncements directly resulted in attacks against certain ethnic groups, they constituted an incitement to violence which warrants government investigation and sanction. In November 1993, for example, the minister of local government and member of parliament for Narok, William ole Ntimama, stated that he had "no regrets about the events in Enosupukia [where a group of Maasai had attacked and driven away thousands of Kikuyus living in a predominantly Maasai area] because the Maasai are fighting for their rights."[92] Ntimama was reported to have organized the Maasai attack on his own account: no measures have ever been taken against him to investigate these charges. In 1994, Mr. Kones threatened to lynch and forcibly expel Luo people from Bomet and Kericho districts if they supported the opposition party, FORD-Kenya.[93] In March 1995, Minister Lotodo, while addressing a crowd at Kenyatta stadium in Kitale town, said that all land in Trans Nzoia district belonged to the Kalenjin (Pokot) community and that if other communities living there did not toe the line, they would be flushed out. Shortly after, seven people were killed and several houses

---

[90]"Feeling the Heat?" *Weekly Review* (Nairobi), April 9, 1992, p.3; and "New Spate of Violence," *Weekly Review* (Nairobi), March 13, 1992, p.18.

[91]"Remaining Kikuyu Told to Move Out by Lotodo," *Daily Nation* (Nairobi), November 29, 1993; and "Tensions Rise in W. Pokot," *Daily Nation* (Nairobi), November 30, 1993.

[92]"Minister: 'No Regrets Over Events'," *Daily Nation* (Nairobi), October 20, 1993.

[93]"Wamalwa Wants Kones Arrested," *Daily Nation* (Nairobi), April 6, 1994.

burnt in Kwanza division.[94]   The outbreak of "ethnic" violence shortly after statements such as these was not uncommon.

Although attackers of all ethnic groups were arrested, various charges were disproportionately brought against members of the Kikuyu and other groups who in general had borne the brunt of the attacks. Often, Kalenjin and Maasai individuals accused of serious offenses, including murder, were released on bail despite continuing disturbances. Since the site of the clash areas was outside the capital, Nairobi, charges and trials were often brought to the local courts in those areas. Away from the international and national scrutiny that pertains to the Nairobi courts, the government was more easily able to criminalize and further disempower some of those it had displaced.

For example, a number of Kikuyus were prosecuted for the crime of "oathing" or weapons possession around the Nakuru area, while similar reports from the Kalenjin community were never investigated. Oathing is an integral part of the history of resistance in Kenya. In the Kenyan context, oathing represents a powerful and significant means for organizing violence.[95] Following the clashes, there were reports of oathing being performed by both Kikuyus and Kalenjins. Many of the Kalenjin warriors who did the attacking reportedly had taken oaths to drive away the non-Kalenjins from the Rift Valley. Oaths among the Kikuyu community were to defend themselves against the Kalenjin attackers and to ensure that the Kikuyu were not driven from the Rift Valley Province. It was also rumored that the oath allows its adherents to retaliate against fellow Kikuyu who leave or sell their land in the Rift Valley Province. In October 1995, fifty-seven of sixty-three Kikuyus who had been arrested in December 1994 and charged with membership in an illegal organization, oathing, and plotting to kill members of the Kalenjin community were convicted. Since 1994, the Catholic Justice and Peace Commission has been providing legal counsel to some forty people, predominantly Kikuyu, who were arrested and charged with allegedly organizing or participating

---

[94]"Pokot Elders Demand Border Review," *Clashes Update* (Nairobi: NCCK), no.41, June 30, 1996, pp.1-2.

[95]During the MauMau struggle for independence, fighters swore oaths that bound them to fight British colonial rule to their death. Ordinary citizens who provided food and shelter to the MauMau fighters also took these oaths, and the effect was that the British colonial government was never able to infiltrate the MauMau movement. Anyone found to betray such an oath, which is performed in complete secrecy, was killed. Oathing had been made an offense under colonial rule. Tabitha Kanogo, *Squatters and the Roots of Mau Mau, 1905-63*, (Nairobi: Heinemann Kenya Ltd., 1987), p.133.

in unlawful meetings. All those charged were either displaced or people who had been working with them. Cases of weapons possession also continue to be pursued against Kikuyus in the Nakuru area.[96] However, the same charges have not been brought against those members of the Kalenjin community responsible for oathing or possessing weapons.

The government has also brought politically-motivated charges against members of the Luhya community. In Western Province, some of the displaced from the Luhya community in Bungoma who had been instrumental in organizing the displaced to form self-help committees to obtain services and facilitate a return to their land were reportedly arrested by the government during a 1995 crackdown against an allegedly clandestine guerrilla movement. In early 1995, the government announced that two guerrilla groups were plotting from Uganda to overthrow the government by force: the February the Eighteenth Resistance Army (FERA) and the Kenya Patriotic Front. Some forty FERA suspects, who were tortured, only appeared in court after *habeas corpus* petitions were filed on their behalf in March 1995. The blatant irregularities in the FERA trials and the use of torture to obtain guilty pleas reinforced the widespread perception that the government was using this claim to further its political ends. Some of the FERA suspects had been arrested in 1994 and held for a year incommunicado. Most of those arrested came from the areas hard hit by the clashes in Mt. Elgon. The displaced in the Bungoma area told Human Rights Watch/Africa that the crackdown against the alleged FERA members provided the government with an opportunity to go after the leaders of the displaced communities in the area. One displaced Luhya man said,

> after we were displaced, we began to organize ourselves. We had self-help groups to distribute food, to negotiate with the Sabaot (Kalenjin) community. Then the government came and picked our leaders and arrested them. It was meant to disorganize us further. As you can see, we are still displaced after all this time. UNDP did nothing for us all that time.[97]

---

[96]Human Rights Watch/Africa interview with Ernest Murimi, Executive Secretary, Justice and Peace Commission, Catholic Diocese of Nakuru, Nakuru, August 6, 1996.

[97]Human Rights Watch/Africa interview with displaced man (Luhya), Namwele, Bungoma district, Western Province, August 3, 1996.

Among those arrested for being FERA members were some thirty Luhyas who had been displaced by the clashes: ten were arrested from Chebusienya, five from Kimaswa, more than five from Lwakhakha and more than ten from Lwandanyi center.[98] Many of the other displaced camp or center representatives were forced to go underground fearing arrest. Currently, some 300 to 400 families displaced from the clashes still live across the border in Uganda afraid to return. The Special Branch security officers in the area have reportedly told them that they cannot return without their permission.

None of these issues were ever addressed by UNDP in the course of its reintegration program. Instead, UNDP dismissed the incitements to ethnic violence by high-ranking government officials as the acts of individuals separate from government policy. However, justice for those wronged should have been one of UNDP goals because these unresolved issues remain a stumbling block to reconciliation. There were a number of local human rights and legal assistance organizations in Kenya, and UNDP could have approached them to create programs to assist with the legal claims by the internally displaced. UNDP should also have put pressure on the Kenyan government to end its uneven and discriminatory application of the law, and to investigate the findings of the government's own 1992 parliamentary report.

Harassment of the Displaced, Relief Workers and Journalists

During the UNDP program, leaders of displaced communities, local and international NGO representatives, and church officials, were continually obstructed in their activities by local government officials. Displaced persons who attempted to form self-help groups to organize schools or assist their communities were singled out and politically-motivated charges, such as participating in illegal meetings, were brought against them. Access to areas, even those not in security operation zones, was periodically denied at the whim of local government officials to those attempting to assist the displaced or to journalists who tried to report on the situation.

One of the government's tactics was to restrict the flow of information. Reporting on events pertaining to the conflict was made particularly difficult for journalists. There were numerous charges of government harassment of the press for reporting on the clashes including arrests without charge, the bringing of patently political charges such as subversion, police interrogation, and the illegal impounding of issues of publications and newspapers that carried articles on the

---

[98]"Update in Brief" and "FERA Crackdown: Over 400 May Not Return," *Clashes Update*, (Nairobi: NCCK), no. 25, February 28, 1995, pp.3,7,11.

clashes. During the year and a half in which the Security Operation regulations were in effect, the media were denied access to three of the worst-hit areas. According to the former Rift Valley P.C., Ishmael Chelanga, the primary reason for the creation of the security zone was to keep away "those who did not wish us well and those who were spreading rumors, lies, and propaganda."[99] By contrast, there has been a general failure to investigate reports of involvement or collusion of government officials, at all levels of responsibility. At no time has President Moi taken steps to censure or discipline those officials who were responsible for this harassment. Among the incidents reported include:[100]

- In January 1994, the government declared Maela camp a restricted area and banned all NGOs, churches and UNDP officials from visiting the camp. On January 5, a contingent of administration and regular police, on orders of the Naivasha D.O., closed down a medical clinic and a makeshift school and destroyed the shelters of the displaced, ordering them to leave. Local government authorities also pressured church officials to stop a church feeding program for the camp residents. Only after intense international and media pressure did local government authorities abandon their actions against the internally displaced at Maela camp.

- On January 7, 1994, two reporters, Moses Wanyama Masinde and Jeff Mbure and their driver Joshua Mutunga, from the NCCK magazine *Target,* were arrested and held for three days without charge after they visited and interviewed the displaced at Maela camp. While in custody, Mr. Masinde was beaten by the district Criminal Investigation Division (CID) officer Godana Golicha. Their notebooks, cameras, employee identity and press cards were confiscated by the police, and they were accused of inciting the victims in the camp. They were released on bond pending police investigation.

- On January 8, 1994, reporters from the *Daily Nation* were prevented from interviewing Maela camp residents by the local D.O. Two weeks later,

---

[99]See Human Rights Watch/Africa, "Multipartyism Betrayed," p.17.

[100]The information about these events was collected since 1994 from a variety of first-hand interviews with the displaced, NGOs, UNDP officials, as well as press reports and the NCCK bulletin, *Clashes Update.*

representatives from the U.S. Embassy were barred from entering the camp. An Irish priest, Tom O'Neil, who had spoken out against the forced eviction was threatened by the Nakuru D.C. and served with a deportation order.

- On March 16, 1994, Ngumo Kuria, *Standard* newspaper's Nakuru bureau chief and Peter Rianga Makori, a provincial correspondent, were arrested and charged with subversion under section 77 of the Kenya Penal Code for "an act prejudicial to the security of the state" by writing a report "intended or calculated to promote feelings of hatred or enmity between different races or communities in Kenya." They were charged after the publication of an article alleging that nine people had been killed and hundreds of others displaced by renewed "ethnic" fighting in Molo, one of the areas in the Rift Valley worst affected by violence in the previous two years. The published story quoted an eyewitness source who claimed to have seen the violence. Government statements that the incident had not occurred were later confirmed to Human Rights Watch/Africa by clergy assisting the displaced in the area. A week later, the managing editor of the *Standard*, Kamau Kanyanga, and the deputy sub-chief, John Nyaosi, were also charged with subversion for editing an article. All four were granted bail on March 31, 1994.

- In April 1994, two priests, Fr. Stephen Mbugua and Fr. Ndenyere, were arrested after visiting Olenguruone, an area that had been badly affected by the clashes.

- On April 10, 1994, FORD-Kenya Member of Parliament Mukhisa Kituyi was prevented by police from entering a camp for displaced people at Thessalia mission in Kericho district to donate fifteen bags of maize to the 630 residents. The police told him that they had been given instructions by the D.C. not to permit access to the displaced. According to the NCCK, children in the mission had begun to suffer from malnutrition.

- On April 11, 1994, Mutegi Njau, news editor of the *Daily Nation*, and Evans Kanini, Eldoret correspondent, were arrested in Nakuru. They had been summoned to the office of the Rift Valley provincial criminal investigations officer to answer questions relating to an article entitled "Clashes: Bishops Condemn the Govt," published in the April 4 edition of the paper. The article had quoted a displaced clash victim from Burnt

Forest claiming that he had seen a government helicopter transporting Kalenjin attackers land on the farm of an unnamed "prominent Rift Valley politician" shortly before residents of nearby Rurigi farm were attacked and driven from their homes. Mr. Njau was charged with subversion and then released on bail.

- *Daily Nation* correspondent Austin Kiguta, based in Laikipia, was interrogated by police in mid-1994 and made to record a statement after he wrote an article on property destruction on an East Laikipia farm.

- In November 1994, the local government administration in parts of Kipkabus turned back a group of displacees when they attempted to return to their farms in the Burnt Forest area. Most of those turned back were living in the NCCK community center in Eldoret.

- On November 29, 1994, eight elders were arrested in Maela camp and interrogated by the police after they questioned a screening process being conducted by UNDP and the government to distinguish genuine clash victims displaced from Enosupukia.

- On November 27, 1994, twelve Kikuyu clash victims from Maela were arrested and charged for allegedly participating in an illegal meeting.

- In late December 1994, UNDP and the international NGO Medecins sans Frontieres (Spain) officials were denied access to Maela camp after forced government dispersals of some 2,000 displaced, despite the fact that the UNDP officer had a letter from the Office of the President allowing entry into Maela. The displaced were transported out of the Rift Valley Province, without notification to UNDP, and left in Central Province in the middle of the night on Christmas eve. An American priest, Fr. John Kaiser, who had been working for the Catholic diocese in Maela, was put under house arrest when he protested the action. He was then taken to nearby Naivasha and warned that he would be deported if he attempted to enter the camp again (See section on Forced Dispersals and Expulsions).

- On December 27, 1994, two *Standard* newspaper journalists, Amos Onyatta and photographer Hudson Wainaina, were arrested and held without charge at Maela while covering the forced dispersals.

- In late December/early January 1995, the government destroyed supplies that had been provided by Medecins sans Frontieres (Spain) to the displaced in Central Province who had been forcibly moved by the government from Maela camp.

- In late December 1994, the government told clash victims at the Eldoret NCCK community center to move back to their farms. The Uasin Gishu D.O., Daniel Lotoai, also made it clear that the government would only aid clash victims on their farms and not in centers and camps. As part of this "resettlement scheme," the D.O. immediately banned the camp's management committee, which was made up of members of the displaced and ordered the chief (a government appointee) to draw up a list of the "genuine camp members" and their farms of origin.

- On January 3, 1995, Medecins sans Frontieres (Spain) staff were denied access to visit the displaced in the Burnt Forest area on the grounds that they needed permission to enter.

- On January 12, 1995, D.O. Daniel Lotai forcibly evicted 179 families that had sought refuge at the Eldoret NCCK center for more than nine months. They were left by the side of the road.

- On January 11, 1995, a Kikuyu priest, Fr. Muranga, was arrested in Nakuru and accused of inciting residents at Longonot where recent attacks by approximately 100 Maasai warriors had left some ten people dead, ten houses burned and an unknown number of livestock stolen. No other arrests were made.

- On January 15, 1995, several opposition members of parliament were detained, including Njanga Mungai, Charles Liwali Oyondi, and Francis John Wanyange. They were arrested in Longonot as they were about to attend a church service for the victims of an ethnic clash that had occurred on January 10 at Mai Mahiu in the Rift Valley. They were charged with promoting "warlike" activities and "uttering words with a seditious intent." On January 20, they were denied bail. In mid-February, the charges were dropped.

- In the same month, five Kikuyus from Kanjoya, near Longonot, were arrested and charged for holding an illegal meeting.
- In February 1995, the government barred the Naivasha Catholic parish and three opposition members of parliament from delivering food to the clash victims. Previously, the government had confiscated checks for more than K.shs200,000 [approximately U.S.$3,600 at that time] given by the Catholic diocese of Ngong for school fees to assist the displaced children in the Maela area.

- On February 25, 1995, the U.S. ambassador to Kenya, Aurelia Brazeal, was held for an hour at Kongoni police post near Naivasha on suspicion that she was accompanying opposition party leaders who wanted to visit Maela camp.

- In late July-early August 1995, Judith Wakahiu, a student at the Moi University's Centre for Refugee Studies, was arrested and held without charge for twelve days before being released. Ms. Wakahiu, a member of the university-registered student group, the Moi University Students' Refugee Welfare Club, had been working at Maela camp during the university vacation period assisting the displaced. She was held in the prison at Naivasha and accused of belonging to an illegal organization. While in custody, she was sexually harassed by a police officer. When the director of the Centre for Refugee Studies, Professor John Okumu, made inquiries about her arrest to the police, his house was ransacked by the police, he was accused of managing an illegal organization, and was held without charge in Naivasha prison for several days before being released.

These, and other incidents, indicate that ongoing harassment and intimidation was taking place in the clash areas on a regular basis. UNDP should have seen it as part of its responsibilities to call for government restraint toward the displaced and those working with or reporting on the displaced, and should have worked towards greater access and transparency in the clash areas. Yet UNDP frequently remained silent about government harassment, and in some cases, made excuses for the Kenyan government by dismissing an incident as a misunderstanding or a temporary setback. Its failure to make public pronouncements critical of government actions was matched by a failure to serve even as a back channel advocate by supporting the agencies by providing factual reporting to donor governments which might have been less constrained to make representations to the Kenyan authorities. A worker with the international NGO Medecins sans Frontieres (Spain) noted that several times during the course of the UNDP program, local government officials destroyed their equipment, arrested their staff, or denied them access to areas where the UNDP program was being administered and where they had permission to enter. They felt that they could not rely on UNDP, either at the field or national level, to speak up on their behalf.

Fraudulent Land Transfers, Illegal Occupation, Pressured Land Sales and Exchanges
        A long-term effect of the violence is the lasting alteration of land occupancy and ownership patterns in the areas where the "ethnic" clashes took place, and a significant reduction of the number of non-Kalenjin landholders, particularly in the Rift Valley Province. The government has continued to pursue its policies of removing certain ethnic groups from the ethnic clash areas by allowing and cooperating in the illegal expropriation of land owned primarily by Kikuyus, Luhyas, and Luos. The increased possession of land by Kalenjins and Maasai in the Rift Valley benefits the Moi government by allowing it to cater to the sentiments of ethnic nationalism among its supporters: it expects their political support by claiming to have got "their" land back and for increasing their economic wealth. In the meantime, thousands of people with title deeds or mortgage notes have been rendered virtually destitute because of their ethnicity.
        In some cases, the land has been completely occupied. In others, the boundaries have been illegally moved to expand the farms of neighboring Kalenjins onto parts of the land of the displaced. In other cases, those kept from their land are being offered sums significantly below market value for their farms. Those who refuse to sell are given warnings by their Kalenjin neighbors that a time will come when they will not only have to sell, but will have to accept the price given to them by Kalenjins. Other non-Kalenjins have exchanged land with people who are willing to take their plot in return for land in another province. In some areas, local Kalenjin authorities have explicitly instructed clash victims to exchange their land with Kalenjins from outside the Rift Valley. For example, in Tapsagoi, a local Kalenjin chief threatened renewed violence unless the non-Kalenjins, who had fled their land after an attack by Kalenjins, exchanged it with Kalenjins, which is in violation of the Land Control Board rules.[101]
        Government officials have also not hesitated to misuse their legal authority to expropriate land under the guise of exercising "eminent domain,"

---

[101]Human Rights Watch/Africa, *Divide and Rule*, p.78.

which allows the government to take over land for the public interest under limited circumstances. In September 1993, the minister for local government, William ole Ntimama, a Maasai who has led the majimbo calls, declared an area in his district a trust land for the Narok County Council. His action was then reinforced by Minister for Environment and Natural Resources John Sambu, who told residents of the forty-four kilometer area that they had to move, because the land would soon be gazetted as a protected area. Not coincidentally, the area's 15,600 inhabitants were Kikuyu. Most had purchased land from Maasai leaders in the 1960s. They believed that they were being harassed for not having supported KANU in the election.

Those displaced who attempt to report the illegal occupation or transfer of their land to the government are sent futilely from one office to the next until they finally are forced to give up. The government is well aware that many of the displaced landholders are poor and unaware of their legal rights, making it unlikely that these transactions will ever be challenged. The government has taken no steps to address the irregularities in land ownership and sales resulting from the violence, portraying the problems as mere contract disputes that need to be dealt with among the affected individuals.

In Olenguruone, Nakuru district, in the Rift Valley Province, Kikuyu landowners are discovering that their title deeds have been transferred without their knowledge into the possession of Kalenjin owners by the Commissioner of Lands in Nakuru. The government has also taken no steps to discipline those civil servants in the land offices who are illegally altering land title deeds to transfer land into the hands of Kalenjins. In 1939, the colonial government settled some 4,000 Kikuyu squatters on the land, which had originally been part of Maasai land. Olenguruone was one of the most affected areas during the clashes, and most of those driven off their land in 1992 and 1993 still remain displaced. One Kenyan characterized Olenguruone as "Kenya's West Bank," referring to the contested Israeli/Palestinian area. Few, if any, Kikuyus from the area are returning to their land because of security fears. Increasingly, the likelihood of their return is being further diminished because of illegal land transfers that are revoking their titles.

Human Rights Watch/Africa interviewed several displaced Kikuyu who inadvertently discovered that their title deeds have been illegally altered by the Commission of Lands. According to lawyer Mirugi Kariuki, "the Land Control Board has become an instrument of control for the government to further its discriminatory policies. The government cannot claim that it is not aware of this because such a process cannot take place without the knowledge of the D.O. in the area."[102] One displaced Kikuyu man told Human Rights Watch/Africa:

> I owned plot number 938 in Chegamba village in Olenguruone. I was chased off my land during the ethnic clashes and the original title deed was burnt. In February 1996, I decided to get a copy of the deed. I went to the Commission of Land, and there I found that the title deed had been transferred in 1994 into the name of a Kalenjin by the name of David Kipgetich Maritim (national ID number 1646-66011/69). I have never sold my land. I complained at the land office and was told to look for a lawyer to help me. I tried to report it to the Criminal Investigation Division and to the Police. They told me to take it to the courts. How can I? I have no money to even get an affidavit.[103]

One twenty-nine-year-old Luhya man who owns a six-acre plot in Chemundi, Western Province, spoke to Human Rights Watch/Africa about his experience. He was attacked on April 4, 1992, and forced to flee. For three years, he sought refuge in a number of nearby towns, until it was safe enough for him to return to his land in September 1995. Since January 1993, a quarter of his plot has been illegally occupied by his Kalenjin (Sabaot) neighbor. He said:

> I have been trying to get my land back without any success since 1993. I reported the illegal occupation to the assistant chief, Patrick Cherokoni, who told me to see the village headman, Elijah Tenge. When I went to him, he told me that there was nothing that he could do and to go and see the assistant chief. The assistant chief told me to see the D.O. I saw the D.O. in February 1993 who sent me to the subchief. I went back to the D.O. in March 1993 and then again in August 1993. Finally, I gave up. I even tried to get the village elders to help me come to a solution, but the Sabaots [Kalenjins] refused. Nothing has

---

[102]Human Rights Watch/Africa interview with Mirugi Kariuki, lawyer, Nakuru, August 7, 1996.

[103]Human Rights Watch/Africa interview with displaced man (Kikuyu), Elburgon, Nakuru district, Rift Valley Province, August 6, 1996.

happened. I am still able to plant on the rest of my land. But I always make sure that there are other Bukusus [Luhyas] here when I am on my land. We still cannot risk going back alone.[104]

Another fifty-three-year-old Luhya man who was displaced from his land in 1992 in Western Province has been staying with relatives about one hour from his land. He tried to return to his land once in December 1994, but was attacked by his Kalenjin neighbors. He has not attempted to reside on his land since then, and he is aware that his neighbors have illegally occupied the land:

> Three acres of my land are being ploughed by my neighbor Ekonya arap Sioi and his two sons. When I have tried to speak with them or stop them, they tell me to leave or they will have me beaten up. I went to the Cheskaki police post, and they told me to go to the headman, Peter Matanda. The headman came to the land with me and even saw them ploughing it. He told me to talk to the subchief, Patrick Cherokoni. I spoke to him, and I also told the police again. They told me to go to the D.O. The D.O. told me to go to the Land Registration Officer, Mr. Muhanji, in Bungoma. I paid Kshs.1,200 [approx. U.S.$ 22] for the transportation to go to Bungoma. The Land Registration Officer came and saw them on the land. They even confronted my neighbor and told him that this was my land and he should not be using it. Then, they asked me for Kshs.2,000 [approx. U.S. $36] to pay for their transportation back to Bungoma. They wanted a bribe. Now, there is nothing more that I can do. I work in a dispensary here. I have a wife and eight children to support. I also have a title deed to land that used to support us. Now I have nothing but that. My house is destroyed, and my land has been taken.[105]

Driven by financial desperation and a belief that the government will never allow them to return to their land, some of the displaced have sold their land

---

[104]Human Rights Watch/Africa interview with former displaced man (Luhya), Namwele, Bungoma district, Western Province, August 3, 1996.

[105]Human Rights Watch/Africa interview with displaced man (Luhya), Namwele, Bungoma district, Western Province, August 3, 1996.

at rates far below market price. One displaced person in Western Province told Human Rights Watch/Africa:

> I sold eighteen acres at a cheap price because I never thought that I would be able to return and the land was the only thing that I had. If I was going to start my life again elsewhere, I needed the money. I sold it at Kshs. 30,000 [approximately U.S.$ 545] per acre.[106]

The market rate in that area is Kshs. 50,000 [U.S. $909] per acre, resulting in a sizable loss of approximately U.S. $6,500 for the eighteen-acre plot.

Another forty-five-year-old displaced Luhya women with eight children told Human Rights Watch/Africa:

> I came from Koborom in Mt. Elgon. In 1991, I was chased from my land. Our house was looted, broken, three of our neighbors were killed. The Sabaots [Kalenjins] who attacked told us to leave because this was their land. Twenty people tried to return there shortly afterwards, but every time they fixed their houses, things were removed. Every time they planted things, the crops were pulled up. They were told not to come up the mountain [Mt. Elgon]. If it was just the Sabaots, then we could resist this. But the police also support this. When we report these incidents, suspects are arrested and then immediately released. Now the Sabaots want to buy the land at a cheap price. One woman I know whose husband was killed in clashes in Kaboromo sold her six-acre plot for Kshs. 30,000 [approximately U.S. $545]. In this area, we usually sell one acre—one acre—between Kshs 45,000 to 60,000 [approximately U.S. $800 to $1,000]. What could she do? She was lame and had nine children to support once her husband was killed.[107]

---

[106]Human Rights Watch/Africa interview with former displaced man (Luhya), Sirisia, Bungoma district, Western Province, August 3, 1996.

[107]Human Rights Watch/Africa interview with displaced woman (Luhya), Sirisia, Bungoma district, Western Province, August 3, 1996.

In Olenguruone, Nakuru district, in the Rift Valley Province, land owned by Kikuyu displaced is being sold at throwaway prices. Generally, the local government administration in this area has not been of assistance to the displaced. One Kikuyu man told Human Rights Watch/Africa, "six acres of land in this area would usually be sold at Kshs 600,000 [approximately U.S.$ 11,000] . But I know someone who sold six acres here for Kshs 70,000 [approximately U.S. $1,300]. Since the clashes, Kikuyus know that they cannot return to that land, so some are selling it.[108]

In other cases, the displaced have exchanged their land for land elsewhere. In the Mount Elgon area, those Luhyas with land on the slopes of the mountain have exchanged plots with Kalenjins who own land lower down the slopes even though the land higher up the mountain is more fertile. A formerly displaced Luhya man who had exchanged his land for land lower down Mt. Elgon told Human Rights Watch/Africa: "I swapped land with the son of Eliah Cheriot even though the land I got was less fertile because I knew that if I took this land, at least I would be able to live in peace."[109] A formerly displaced Luhya man told Human Rights Watch/Africa:

> I was driven off my eight acres of land at Kamaneru on April 8, 1992. My house was burned, my six cows and two sheep were taken. Everything that I owned was lost. I stayed at Kapkateny working day jobs to make some money to support my wife and six children. I tried to go back four times. Each time, the Kalenjins there told me that they did not want to see me back there. Now, I have exchanged my land with a Kalenjin. I am not happy with this exchange. He has got a bigger plot. But this was the best option. If I continued doing casual labor, I would have had to work harder, and I would have had to pay rent. This way I can at least support myself.[110]

---

[108]Human Rights Watch/Africa interview with displaced man (Kikuyu), Elburgon, Nakuru district, Rift Valley Province, August 6, 1996.

[109]Human Rights Watch/Africa interview with former displaced man (Luhya), Lwakhakha market, Bungoma district, Western Province, August 3, 1996.

[110]Human Rights Watch/Africa interview with former displaced man (Luhya), Kapkateny, Mt. Elgon district, Western Province, August 3, 1996.

The government is slowly, but surely, consolidating and legalizing the illegal gains from the "ethnic" violence in such a way as to reduce permanently land ownership of certain ethnic groups in the areas which it has promised to its supporters. This constitutes a constructive forced eviction of the individuals who are coerced into relinquishing their property and their homes. Although this process was well underway during the UNDP program, no steps were taken by UNDP to address the illegal land appropriation. UNDP should have put pressure on the government to end these illegal land transactions and provided assistance to the displaced to challenge these transactions in court.

Forced Dispersals and Expulsions

To ensure that large gatherings of clash victims were not easily visible to visiting diplomats, the media or human rights groups, local government officials dispersed camps of the internally displaced without any consideration of where these victims could go. One method that was frequently used was to announce to the victims, despite evidence to the contrary, that it was safe to return to their land. In other cases, where the displaced would not leave voluntarily, local government officials, with the assistance of the police, would forcibly disperse camps of displaced people without providing adequate assistance or security to permit them to return to their land. The result of the dispersals, which continued even in 1996, has made it virtually impossible to identify those who were displaced from their land by the "ethnic" violence today. The violence and the ensuing government harassment has condemned a formerly self-sufficient and productive sector of the economy to permanent dispossession and poverty. Many are renting homes or living on hired land. Others have become part of the urban poor, either unemployed or working as day laborers who receive barely enough to survive. Many of the displaced are farmers by occupation who did not receive much formal education or training in skills of the salaried sector. As a result, some of the displaced have been reduced to begging or crime in order to survive. In recent years, there has been an alarming rise in the number of street children in Kenya. Among them are many children who were displaced and dispossessed by the clashes.[111]

There were expectations that government harassment of the internally displaced would cease, particularly once the UNDP program began. However, this proved not to be the case. The crowning incident of government disregard for the

---

[111]See Human Rights Watch, *Juvenile Injustice: Police Abuse and Detention of Street Children in Kenya*," (New York: Human Rights Watch/Children's Rights Project, June 1997), pp.18-19.

internally displaced, UNDP and the international community took place in December 1994 at a camp called Maela when the government forcibly expelled the residents. This lent credence to the charges that the government was clearing the Rift Valley Province of certain ethnic groups.

The predominantly Kikuyu displaced population at Maela camp had sought refuge there after being attacked on its land at Enosupukia, Narok district, by a group of Maasai in October 1993. Since that time, they had been living at Maela camp in squalid conditions under plastic sheeting on church grounds. The overcrowding had led to shortages of food, water, and medical supplies. Incidents of government harassment of the displaced at this camp periodically occurred as did statements by Maasai leaders that the displaced at Maela would never be permitted to return to their land.

In the early hours of the morning of December 24, 1994, administration police and KANU youth wingers raided the camp of Maela which housed approximately 10,000 predominantly Kikuyu people who had sought refuge after being attacked at Enosupukia in October 1993.[112] Without notice, the government officials razed the camp and transported some 2,000 residents to Central Province (the area regarded as the "traditional" home of the Kikuyus), and proceeded to

---

[112]Following independence, Kikuyu farmers began settling among the Maasai pastoralists in the Enosupukia area. In 1977, the area was designated a land adjudication area, and the government began to issue title deeds to purchasers. Many of those who bought land were Kikuyu. At the time, Maasai leaders welcomed the Kikuyu settlers and community relations thrived. Following the calls for a multiparty system, Maasai leaders from the area began to call for the expulsion of the Kikuyu from this area. In August 1993, William ole Ntimama, KANU Minister for Local Government and Maasai himself, declared the region "trust land" and illegally conferred upon local authorities the power to evict people regarded as squatters. Mr. Ntimama began to make public statements referring to the Kikuyu as "aliens" or "foreigners" and calling for their expulsion from the indigenous Maasai land. Tensions continued to heighten and, in October 1993, violence occurred displacing both Maasai and Kikuyu farmers, but resulting primarily in the displacement of an estimated 30,000 Kikuyu. In a parliamentary debate following the incident, Minister Ntimama said that he had no regrets about the events in Enosupukia because "Kikuyus had suppressed the Maasai, taken their land and degraded their environment." He stated "we had to say enough is enough. I had to lead the Maasai in protecting our rights." The government has never taken any steps to hold Mr. Ntimama responsible for incitement to violence, nor have the displaced been able to return to Enosupukia to date. "Deception, Dispersal and Abandonment: A Narrative Account on the Displacement of Kenyans from Enoosupukia and Maela based upon Witness, Church/NGO and Media Accounts," prepared for the Ethnic Clashes Network under the auspices of the Kenyan National Council of NGOs, Nairobi, January 16, 1995, p.10.

question them about their ethnicity and ancestral background. Families were separated as they were herded into about twenty trucks which had been fueled from a UNDP petrol account (which was later closed after UNDP discovered this fact). Each truck was crammed with approximately one hundred people. Initially, the displaced were not provided with food or shelter. The relocation was done late at night without notification or the participation of UNDP.

The remaining residents of Maela were left without shelter, and UNDP and the international NGO Medecins sans Frontieres (Spain) were denied access to Maela, despite the fact that the UNDP officer had a letter from the office of the president allowing entry into Maela. UNDP was informed that this resettlement was in keeping with the President's promise to resettle the genuine victims of Maela before Christmas. Some 200 "genuine" victims, as defined by the government, were relocated to a government-owned farm near Maela called MoiNdabi and each given two acres. The land at MoiNdabi, which used to be part of a larger farm administered by the government Agricultural Development Cooperation (ADC), is less productive than the land the displaced were forced from in Enosupukia, and water, shelter and sanitation facilities were non-existent when they arrived.[113]

The other Maela camp residents, considered "non-genuine" displacees by the government, were dumped at three different locations in Central Province in the middle of the night and left to fend for themselves. At Ndaragwa, the displaced were left by the side of the road with no shelter and practically no belongings. At Ol Kalou, they were left between the railway line and the main road. At Kiambu, they were dropped at Kirigiti Stadium. Several days later, the makeshift camp at Kirigiti was destroyed in a police raid at 3:00 am, leaving the twice displaced once again without shelter. The displaced were ordered to line up and were loaded on trucks without being informed of where they were to be taken. Those who resisted were beaten and forcibly thrown into the trucks. The government denied any harassment or beatings. None of those forcibly displaced to Central Province were returned by the government or UNDP to the area they came from in the Rift Valley Province. Furthermore, the government officials responsible for the brutality

---

[113]In August 1996, Human Rights Watch/Africa visited MoiNdabi where the resettled families still live. Residents were apprehensive about speaking to Human Rights Watch/Africa on the grounds that they might get into trouble with the local government authorities, or perhaps even lose the land they had been given. While the land is not as fertile as the land that the MoiNdabi residents once owned, they did express gratitude that they were no longer displaced. As far as Human Rights Watch/Africa can determine, these 200 residents are the only ones who have been resettled by the government.

against the displaced have never been disciplined.[114] (See section on Abandoning the Displaced).

Although the blatant disregard by the Kenyan government of the UNDP program was obstructing reintegration efforts, UNDP continued to downplay the government's detrimental role. Even after the dispersal of Maela camp, UNDP insisted that this was a minor aberration rather than a symptom of a larger problem with the government. UNDP's handling of the affair drew condemnation from all sides. The NGO community and the political opposition criticized UNDP for its unwillingness to stand up for the displaced throughout, noting that they had warned UNDP that the government was not committed genuinely to the return of all. David Whaley, UNDP resident representative to Kenya at that time, did little to allay these concerns when, during a meeting of donors convened on January 4, 1995 to discuss the Maela incident, he termed the forced relocation a "hiccup" in the larger reintegration program.[115] Even some working on the UNDP program at the time found this assessment hard to swallow. David Round-Turner, former policy advisor with the UNDP Displaced Persons Program, recalled: "That was no hiccup. It was a major gastric upset. It was a slap in the face to UNDP."[116]

The UNDP's misportrayal of the situation appeared to be a problem throughout. In December 1994, barely two weeks before Maela took place, UNDP wrote to Human Rights Watch/Africa in response to concerns raised by Human Rights Watch/Africa about the UNDP program. The letter, which once again put a positive spin on the situation, without even a hint of the problems being experienced, stated: "we have also received increasingly strong support from most political parties and other parts of Kenyan society and think that our approach has been sensitive and timely in implementation."[117] Meanwhile, Ernest Murimi of the Catholic Justice and Peace Commission based in Nakuru told Human Rights Watch/Africa "It was no surprise to us when the government cleared Maela. We

---

[114]"Deception, Dispersal and Abandonment." Kenyan National Council of NGOs, Nairobi, January 16, 1995.

[115]Ibid., p.20.

[116]Human Rights Watch/Africa interview with David Round-Turner, former Policy Advisor, UNDP Displaced Persons Program, Nairobi, August 26, 1996.

[117]Letter from Killian Kleinschmidt, then Senior Technical Advisor, UNDP Displaced Persons Programme, Nairobi, to Binaifer Nowrojee, Human Rights Watch/Africa, December 13, 1994.

knew that the Kenyan government was trying to disperse them before this happened. Mark Cassidy [UNDP Field Officer] knew this too. I told Mark Cassidy that this was going to happen. The problem with UNDP was that it trusted the government too much."[118]

The forced dispersals at Maela brought the UNDP program to a virtual standstill, and prompted it to uncharacteristic public criticisms. UNDP protested the dispersals in a letter to the government and publicly disassociated itself from the operation in Maela, stating that UNDP was committed to protecting those who had been relocated.[119] UNDP's criticism prompted President Moi to attack the agency for criticizing the "reintegration" process at Maela, accusing it of not delivering the U.S.$20 million it had pledged to raise for the project, and warning UNDP not to interfere in internal affairs.[120] On January 10, David Whaley, former resident representative to Kenya, met with President Moi and UNDP reiterated its concerns: President Moi denied involvement in the forced dispersal. In a meeting with Human Rights Watch/Africa in February 1995, UNDP admitted that serious violations of human rights had taken place, however, they were not willing to place any conditionalities on the continuation of the UNDP program since they believed that the government was looking for a way to stop the program and UNDP did not want to give the government any excuse to do so. David Whaley, in that meeting, also reiterated that until recently the program had been very positive.[121]

---

[118]Human Rights Watch/Africa interview with Ernest Murimi, Executive Secretary, Justice and Peace Commission, Catholic Diocese of Nakuru, Nakuru, August 6, 1996.

[119]Human Rights Watch/Africa interview with David Whaley, former UNDP Resident Representative to Kenya and Killian Kleinschmidt, former UNDP Senior Technical Advisor to the Displaced Persons Program, New York, January 12, 1995.

[120]"U.S. Rebukes Kenya Over Treatment of Displaced," Reuters, January 5, 1995; and "Moi Blasts U.N. Agency on Mass Resettlement Reports," Agence France Presse, December 30, 1994.

[121]Human Rights Watch/Africa interview with David Whaley, former UNDP Resident Representative to Kenya and Killian Kleinschmidt, former UNDP Senior Technical Advisor to the Displaced Persons Program, New York, January 12, 1995.

One diplomat said "After Maela, UNDP went into a holding pattern. Nothing much was done."[122] Eleven months after Maela, the program was ended in November 1995, with a government agreement in principle to incorporate activities in favor of displaced persons in its development program plan, the Social Dimensions of Development—which would receive UNDP support.[123] UNDP Resident Representative to Kenya, Frederick Lyons, announced that some 180,000 of an estimated 250,000 displaced had returned to their land.[124] Requests by Human Rights Watch/Africa for a regional breakdown of this figure were never answered by UNDP.

---

[122]Human Rights Watch/Africa interview with a diplomat (name withheld by request), Nairobi, August 8, 1996.

[123]The Social Dimensions of Development program is a government-proposed development plan which encompasses social programmes in areas such as health, water, education, family planning, support for women and children, micro-economic activities, environmental protection, and emergency relief.

[124]"Clashes: shs.600m Spent," *Daily Nation* (Nairobi), June 17, 1996.

8. MISSED OPPORTUNITIES:
AN ASSESSMENT OF THE UNDP PROGRAM

"Time has healed the wounds, not UNDP"
—former UNDP employee, Nakuru, August 8, 1996

UNDP deserves credit for a initiating a program, for creating a national forum for dialogue, providing relief assistance to the displaced, and serving as a calming intermediary in a tense situation which assisted thousands of Kenyans to return to their homes. These achievements should in no way be discounted, and Human Rights Watch/Africa recognizes the contributions of this program that facilitated reintegration. However, the Displaced Persons Program in Kenya was not without its shortcomings. The UNDP resident representative to Kenya, Frederick Lyons, has pointed out:

> Look at the experience as a whole. Twelve million dollars were spent eventually and that figure corresponds with the 170,000 to 180,000 resettled. It is a big sum of money. Not everything was done in the best possible way, but we have learned from the process. We played a positive role in building bridges between the communities, the donors and the local and national government. That success is reflected in what happened. Things have calmed down. It is easy to be pessimistic—but if you look at the glass as half full, we did make a difference. UNDP served as a useful conduit and managed as a facilitator at a time when tensions were high.[125]

While UNDP cannot be held responsible for the Kenyan government's recalcitrance, it does bear some responsibility for the thousands who remain displaced today. There are a number of identifiable factors that could have strengthened UNDP's contribution. UNDP did not put into place a working agreement with the government setting out basic operating conditions for the program. UNDP misread the situation and did not put into place mechanisms to guard against government abuse. UNDP did not prioritize data collection. In the context of forced dispersals by the government, the absence of a monitoring and reporting function meant that there was no sustained follow-up or means of

---

[125]Human Rights Watch/Africa interview with Frederick Lyons, UNDP Resident Representative to Kenya, Nairobi, August 22, 1996.

identifying those displaced who were expelled from identifiable camp-like situations. UNDP also did not play a vigorous and outspoken advocacy and protection role to protect the displaced against human rights abuses. UNDP was silent on the need for accountability, and too ready to accept and to propound arguments that only a few officials were involved as an alternative to confronting the government's betrayal of the very premise of its program. Its program did not support and strengthen the local NGO community. As a result of these omissions and the government's obstruction, UNDP was forced to end the program prematurely without addressing the long-term solutions, including land reform, leaving thousands abandoned. An examination of these factors, if acted on by UNDP, may avoid the same errors from being repeated in programs elsewhere.

What was required in Kenya was a UNDP program that moved from emergency relief to durable solutions: a program that blended immediate assistance and protection needs with long-term rehabilitation and development strategies. UNDP should have coordinated the relief assistance side with the NGOs already providing aid on the ground, while concentrating primarily on addressing the fundamental political and human rights impediments that needed to be removed to ensure a successful transition to full reintegration. Working within a highly volatile situation where accusations of government involvement were rife, UNDP also needed to distance itself somewhat from the government and play a watchdog role to prevent and address government abuses against the displaced. Although ultimate responsibility for returning the displaced to their land lay with the Kenyan government, one of UNDP's roles should have been that of an advocate for the displaced to press for conditions conducive to return.

UNDP proceeded as if all that was necessary was to provide relief supplies to allow people to return to rebuild their homes and cultivate their land, while doing nothing more than acknowledging the causes of the displacement—and the attendant violations that needed addressing. An international humanitarian worker who worked with the displaced said:

> this program seemed to be modeled on a similar program done in 1992 for drought and famine victims. Not only did we think that program had failed because it was a bed of corruption, but here you had a situation where the government had created and benefitted from the violence. Anyone could have told you that

this was not going to be the same as reintegrating drought victims.[126]

Various UNDP documents on the displaced program for Kenya acknowledge and recognize this fact, citing the importance of addressing a variety of human rights, rule of law, protection, and development issues. But ultimately these critical factors were neglected in the implementation phase of the program. Throughout, UNDP remained highly involved in the emergency relief end of things—along with the NGO and church groups—but never seriously took on the protection or development roles for which it was best equipped, both as the lead agency in this case, and as a part of the larger U.N. organization with expertise in these areas upon which it should have drawn..

The 1994 (second) Rogge report, which was issued at the mid-point of the program, contributed to the misleading impression that things were going better than they actually were and that reintegration was proceeding at a brisk pace with government blessings. Many in the local NGO community believe that the second Rogge report missed the opportunity for UNDP to reassess its direction at a critical time when it could have made a difference. Ernest Murimi of the Catholic Justice and Peace Commission believes that "in the second report, Rogge rushed. He seemed to have preconceived ideas about what was happening. He also threw out the figures of those resettled without consultation. Those numbers did not reflect what we were seeing on the ground. By 1994, UNDP had become an arm of the government."[127] Donors also expressed concerns that the Rogge report lacked a detailed assessment of UNDP itself and that the report's recommendations were not feasible because of a lack of capacity within the UNDP. Had the 1994 Rogge report sounded a stronger warning about the problems in the program at that time, it is possible that could have underscored to UNDP what it needed to do at a time when it could have made a difference.

The manner in which UNDP implemented the Kenyan program had several detrimental effects. First, the UNDP program allowed the government to deflect international criticism of its ongoing policies of ethnic discrimination and to obtain donor and investment funding on the grounds that it was reintegrating the

---

[126]Human Rights Watch/Africa interview with international relief worker (name withheld by request), Nairobi, July 30, 1996.

[127]Human Rights Watch/Africa interview with Ernest Murimi, Executive Secretary, Justice and Peace Commission, Catholic Diocese of Nakuru, Nakuru, August 6, 1996.

displaced (all the while continuing to obstruct reintegration and institutionalize the new land distribution through manipulation of the land registry). Throughout the program, the Kenyan government consistently used the UNDP program as a basis for asserting to the international community that the situation had normalized, while continuing to pursue its policy of ethnic persecution. Instead of mobilizing sustained multilateral pressure on the Kenyan government by raising ongoing concerns with donors, UNDP's approach was instrumental in contributing to the impression that all was going well with reintegration. At a London Investors' Conference in November 1994, the reason cited by bilateral and multilateral donors for why a successful meeting could be held on investment in Kenya was the government's improvement in the handling of communities affected by the ethnic violence.[128] In the closing statement of the Consultative Group meeting of Kenya's donors on December 15 and 16, 1994, the chair noted that there had been "positive developments" with respect to ethnic tensions and human rights issues.[129]

Second, the UNDP program spent an enormous amount of money, which in retrospect, might have been used more effectively had it been applied differently. Although the proposed budget for the program was initially U.S.$20 million, eventually only some U.S.$12 million was raised.[130] In addition to a UNDP revolving fund of U.S. $800,000, donor assistance to UNDP for the program was pledged by, among others, the governments of Austria, Denmark, Finland, Japan, the Netherlands, Sweden, the United Kingdom (U.K.), the U.S., and the European

---

[128]Letter from David Whaley, former UNDP Resident Representative to Kenya to Mr. W. Kimilat, Permanent Secretary, Kenyan Government, December 27, 1994.

[129]In this regard, UNDP adds: "The issue of IDPs [internally displaced persons] in the Rift Valley and Western Kenya was important for donors from 1993 to 1995, but it was not the determining factor in decisions on aid and investment. Structural adjustment was the priority. This was the critical aspect of the Kenyan situation discussed at the Consultative Group meeting of 15 December 1994. The statement of Chair [sic] of that meeting, in voicing the generally accepted view that there had been improvements in the human rights area as well as a lessening of ethnic tension, contributed to the decision to release external funding but it did not determine it. The sudden reversal of budgetary policy that occurred in the week following the CG [Consultative Group] meeting was a more serious development for most donors than the tragedy at Maela. It was certainly the key factor that led to a change of heart on the part of the World Bank and the IMF [International Monetary Fund]." See Appendix: UNDP Response, p.7.

[130]Human Rights Watch/Africa interview with Frederick Lyons, UNDP Regional Representative to Kenya, Nairobi. August 22, 1996.

Union (E.U.). Appeals were made to the international community, but donors were slow to respond, privately citing reservations about the Kenyan government's commitment to ending the clashes. Similarly, church and local relief organizations working with the displaced, while welcoming the efforts begun by UNDP, expressed strong misgivings about the government's commitment. UNDP never managed to raise the full amount it had anticipated from donors. Later, as the program floundered, some donors who had previously committed funding withheld their pledges.[131] Ultimately, when the program ended in September 1995, UNDP had to return some money to donors.[132]

Third, UNDP's long-term contribution to addressing the issues raised by the ethnic violence and the displacement is questionable. The UNDP displaced persons program left a Kenya that is as easily able to explode with ethnic violence in the future as it did in the early 1990s—if that suits the government. An examination of the situation of the displaced in Kenya today differs very little from the situation described in the second Rogge report of 1994. While there are thousands who have returned to their land in some areas, there are still thousands who farm on their land in the day and sleep elsewhere at night, fearing reprisals if they return to their land. There are thousands of others who cannot return to their land at all because of anticipated or actual violence or because their land has been illegally occupied, sold or transferred. There are still thousands more who have become urban slum dwellers. The grievances that allowed for the manipulation of ethnic tensions have not been addressed, nor have the justice and land issues that are key to finding sustainable solutions.

Fourth, UNDP's silence in the face of continued discrimination against the displaced allowed the government to continue to consolidate its political gains by allowing its supporters to "legalize" and profit from their ill-gotten gains. Even today, land throughout the clash areas continues to be illegally occupied or officially transferred into the possession of Kalenjin and Maasai owners who acquired the land through violence, with the knowledge of local government officials. Fraudulent land sales and transfers have been countenanced by local

---

[131]Following forced relocations of the displaced from Maela camp, pledges of U.S.$556,476 by the U.S. government and U.S.$540,000 by the Swedish government were suspended. Positive indications given by Belgium for U.S.$3 million at the 1994 December Consultative Group meeting were also withdrawn. UNDP, "UNDP Mission Report," April 18-22, 1995, Annex 1.

[132]Human Rights Watch/Africa interview with Frederick Lyons, UNDP Regional Representative to Kenya, Nairobi. August 22, 1996.

government officials, and no steps have ever been taken by the national government to reverse the illegal land transactions that transpired since the ethnic clashes. The displaced who seek redress for the illegal occupation or transfer of their land from local government officials are sent futilely from one office to the next until they are finally forced to give up.

Lastly, UNDP's credibility, independence and impartiality were damaged by this program. The displaced, the NGOs working with them and donors, strongly feel that UNDP colluded with the Kenyan government at the cost of the protection and welfare of the displaced. While UNDP can be credited for coordinating a national program, for bringing together all the actors involved, and even providing relief and assistance that allowed some to return to their land, the program failed to address the fundamental issues critical for long-term development. UNDP failed to create a registration system that would have allowed for sustained monitoring of the displaced; it did not set out explicit terms of agreement with the government as a condition of the program which protected the rights of the displaced; UNDP was reticent to criticize the government's human rights abuses against the displaced or to address the justice and accountability issues arising from the violations; it did not put enough pressure on the Kenyan government to ensure adequate protection to the displaced; it did not support and strengthen the local NGO community; and it failed to address the long-term solutions, such as the underlying tensions of land distribution. UNDP's silence and inaction on these issues greatly damaged its credibility in the eyes of many Kenyans.

A Well-Conceptualized Program

It is commendable that UNDP initiated and created a program to address a situation of internal displacement which was receiving virtually no international assistance. The preparatory stages of the project were consultative with input drawn from other U.N. agencies; the approach to secure the government's agreement for the program was successful; and the strong program document drafted by John Rogge in 1993 set the stage for a program that could have had far-reaching consequences for resolving the Kenyan situation.

Once the approval for the project had been secured from the government, UNDP's stated approach was to create a program that incorporated the input of the displaced, the NGO community and the government, to address the relief, protection and reconciliation needs of the displaced. According to UNDP:

> The U.N. program was based on the principle of the community
> finding its own way back to harmony and coexistence and the
> value of locally initiated rehabilitation and development

activities. It fully recognized the important role of churches and NGOs in the provision of relief, based on their acceptance by the communities and their critical input to the process of reconciliation. On the other hand, the U.N. program also recognized the need for the government to address the issues of security, access, registration and longer term problem—though preferably discreet—donor support and informal monitoring through the United Nations.[133]

No Terms of Agreement with Government

One of the major omissions of the UNDP Displaced Persons Program, identified primarily by the UNDP staff who worked on the program, was that there was no firm agreement signed with the Kenyan government. Government involvement in the program was critical to its success. At no time during the UNDP program in Kenya was there any program document that spelled out the responsibilities of the Kenyan government and bound it to taking certain actions. A former UNDP staff member said:

> There should have been a clear contract with the Kenyan government. But there was not for a number of reasons. From the perspective of UNDP at the central level [New York], this was a confusing and strange project to deal with because this was something new for UNDP. A program that dealt with relief to rehabilitation is not something that UNDP does often. Then, we were also dealing with a volatile situation inside the country. Adding to that, there were no firm donor commitments to finance the program. All these factors made us feel that we needed to step slowly and to appease the Kenyan government at first to get them to be part of the process. We knew that we were dealing with the devil, but we did not want to expose them or ask for accountability because these were the people in power. Our approach was to cool things down first, engage them, and then move to accountability and a national commission of inquiry. This was the right approach, and it got us some distance, and there was some reintegration. But, where there was not or when things went wrong, we had nothing to fall back on—not with the Kenyan government and not with UNDP in New York.

---

[133]See Appendix: UNDP Response, p.2.

> Everything always came back to the fact that we had no working
> agreement.[134]

In its response to Human Rights Watch/Africa, UNDP acknowledged the difficulties this posed and elaborated on the reasons, stating:

> The U.N. team on the ground, including the UNDP Resident
> Representative, would agree that the lack of a formal agreement
> between UNDP and the Government has been criticised as one
> of the factors contributing to the confusion. This confusion
> arose, in part, from the difficulty in reaching agreement with the
> Government, but also the uncertainly over funding that made it
> impossible for UNDP to enter into specific commitments that
> would have allowed it to call for reciprocal formal commitments
> from the Government.[135]

UNDP did, however, use the opportunity presented by the proposals of the National Committee for Displaced Persons (NCDP) to transmit written plans to the government in 1994 for a continued and expanded program. According to UNDP, these were incorporated into the basic agreement between the government and UNDP. However, these were not sufficient replacement for a formal agreement.

The lack of firm operating standards between UNDP and the Kenyan government allowed the government to disregard the UNDP program in ways that suited it and to avoid being held to any minimum standard of responsibility towards the displaced. UNDP should have had an operating agreement with the Kenyan government signed prior to the program, binding the government to certain minimum steps, including free access to the displaced at all times; prior notification of any government movement of the displaced; advanced assessment by the U.N. of any areas designated by the government for reintegration; U.N.-supervised movement of people with advance notice to a reasonable area; no government registration of the displaced without U.N. presence; no government harassment of the displaced; no forcible destruction of camps; and disciplinary actions to be taken against government officials involved in mistreatment of the displaced.

---

[134]Human Rights Watch/Africa telephone interview with former UNDP Displaced Persons Program official (name and location withheld on request), New York, March 12, 1997.

[135]See Appendix: UNDP Response, p.6.

Providing a National Forum for All Actors

One of the roles of the UNDP program was to convene a forum of all agencies involved with the displaced to ensure coordination and guidance on the overall implementation of the program and prevent duplication of efforts. This endeavor was successful in furthering dialogue and reconciliation, as were its efforts to initiate local and regional community meetings to raise issues. These fora allowed the local community representatives, government officials, NGOs and UNDP to regularly interact.

Since the inception of the clashes and prior to the UNDP program, a number of NGOs and church organizations had been assisting the displaced. However, there was little or no coordination or cooperation among the nongovernmental sector, let alone with the international NGOs or the government. Tensions have always run high between the government and the local NGO community, with constant government harassment and intimidation of NGO workers who attempted to assist the displaced.

In July 1994, UNDP set up a National Committee for Displaced Persons (NCDP) which consisted of representatives from the government's Office of the President, donors, UNDP and the local and international nongovernmental community.[136] The stated role of the NCDP working group, chaired by the Office of the President, was to "structure policy to be implemented in defined areas focusing on the district and local government administrations to coordinate and help the NGOs and church groups at the local level implement their programmes and activities."

Although the full NCDP only met twice, it is widely agreed that it was a useful creation on several grounds. First, the NCDP provided a forum for greater exchange of information and afforded the NGOs some measure of protection to raise issues and offer criticism without fear of government retaliation. According

---

[136]Although attendance at the meetings varied, the official membership of the NCDP included representatives from the Kenyan Government's Office of the President and the Vice-President and from the Ministries of Finance, Lands, and Planning and Development. Among the bilateral donors, representatives from the Embassies of the U.S., U.K., Netherlands and Canada were represented. Among multilateral donors, the E.U., WFP, UNIFEM and UNICEF were represented. Among the Kenyan nongovernmental organizations, representatives from the NCCK, the Church Province of Kenya (CPK), the Catholic Secretariat, the Muslim World League, the NGO Council, FIDA-Kenya, Kituo cha Sheria (Legal Aid Center) and Inades Formation were members. Among the international nongovernmental organizations, Oxfam, Action Aid, Medecins sans Frontieres (Spain) and Catholic Relief Services were also members. The International Committee of the Red Cross had observer status.

to Ephraim Kiragu of the NCCK, "the one positive role that UNDP played was to facilitate a forum for the key players to meet. It was the first time that we sat face to face around a table to discuss this issue with the government. And that was useful."[137] Also in agreement was Irungu Houghton of the NGO Council who noted that "the NCDP meetings provided an opportunity for everyone to speak and to raise all issues in a forum. The meetings served as an information gathering and sharing session, and one got a sense of government thinking. The presence of donor countries at the meetings was positive. The donors were there, and the government wanted funding so they could not intimidate people."[138]

Second, the NCDP also created greater transparency on the part of the government, which was called to respond to developments at every meeting. By including government officials in the wider dialogue with all the other actors, the government was forced to cooperate in the reintegration process and had to make the right noises, at least publicly, about the need for peace and reconciliation. Further, even the limited cooperation of the government at the national level meetings sifted down to the local levels, and NGOs working with the displaced in some areas were able to elicit greater cooperation from local government officials, who would otherwise have been wary of cooperating without explicit orders from the national government. "It was constructive to bring in the government," noted Tecla Wanjala, who worked with the displaced in Western Province. "It got some of the local officials who were hostile on board."[139]

The NCDP meetings also engaged and sustained donor interest in the project. One diplomat said:

> UNDP was not very good about keeping the donors appraised
> about what was happening. The lack of information further
> added to our unwillingness to contribute to a program which we
> already thought was problematic. Once Killian Kleinschmidt
> [former UNDP Senior Technical Advisor] came on board, he

---

[137]Human Rights Watch/Africa interview with Ephraim Kiragu, Director, Development Unit, NCCK, Nairobi, August 8, 1996.

[138]Human Rights Watch/Africa interview with Irungu Houghton, National Council of NGOs, Nairobi, August 9, 1996.

[139]Human Rights Watch/Africa interview with Tecla Wanjala, Coordinator, Peace and Development Network (Peace-Net), National Council of NGOs, Nairobi, August 8, 1996.

personally did a lot to ensure that the information flow improved and that the NCDP meetings were a useful forum. It was largely because of his efforts that we donated to the program.[140]

A further benefit of the NCDP meetings was increased communication between the various NGOs. While the NGO contribution towards relief assistance and longer-term reintegration, particularly by the church organizations, has without question been the single most important source of help for most of the displaced, the NGO community was certainly not without its own competitiveness and lack of transparency. As a result, areas were often being serviced by two or more groups, resulting in a duplication of effort in some areas and an absence in others. Since update reports were given on each group's work, the NCDP helped to facilitate the streamlining of NGO efforts and the division of operational areas, and focused greater attention on the neglected areas. The NCDP also mitigated somewhat the competitiveness among the NGO community and allowed for greater information-sharing among the NGOs.

No Comprehensive Data Collection

The collection and documentation of data, while often time-consuming and costly, is an important dimension of dealing with any displacement program. Without access to reliable information and data, it is difficult to assess the needs of the situation or to advance successful strategies. Accurate data can provide an important indicator of how well the program is working and offer an ongoing opportunity to assess whether the program is meeting the needs of the remaining displaced. That said, data on the internally displaced is often difficult to collect. Undertaking a detailed enumeration can even place people at risk in some cases. Notwithstanding these impediments, UNDP has recognized the need for better information systems on the internally displaced.[141]

---

[140]Human Rights Watch/Africa telephone interview with a diplomat (name and location withheld by request), New York, March 13, 1997.

[141]"UNDP recognizes the need for better information systems in IDPs [internally displaced persons]. Apart from registering IDP number and needs, such systems must also record action taken to meet both relief and development requirements. This indispensable data is often neglected in the understandable rush to assist, yet it is the foundation for coherently shaping comprehensive programmes from the activities of different agencies. UNDP will continue to contribute to the building of information systems on IDPs at the country level." "Further Elaboration on Follow-up to Economic and Social Council

Since the beginning of the "ethnic" violence in 1991, the absence of accurate information on the situation has provided an opportunity for the Kenyan government to evade its responsibility to those who remain displaced and made it close to impossible for the NGO community to help many of those who remain off their land. The consequences of the lack of accurate data, both qualitative and quantitative, have been tragic for those who remain displaced in Kenya today. Even if an international program for the displaced was to recommence, there is little or no way to identify or contact many of those who still desperately need help to rebuild their broken lives.

In each of the affected areas, UNDP should have conducted an appraisal as soon as possible to register and determine names and numbers of displaced, the abandoned plot registration number, and the location from where each of the displaced had been forced. Additionally, interviews with the displaced about their needs and conditions would have greatly enhanced UNDP's ability to cater the program to the specific situation. In Kenya, because of the national identity card system, it would have been relatively easy for UNDP to create a national data base using national identity card numbers and the corresponding plot number from which the person had been displaced. In some areas, the local church and NGOs had already begun to use national identity card numbers in order to reduce duplicate registration. However, one could get differing figures from different NGOs in the same areas. UNDP could have given the responsibility for data collection to its field officers who could have obtained all the various estimates, collected names, and sent the information to Nairobi for the creation of a national database. This database would certainly not have been 100 percent accurate, given the fact that UNDP was coming in two years after the violence had begun. Additionally, some of the displaced did not want to be on "lists" and others were dispersed among relatives or were out of the region, and hence could not have been sampled even if UNDP had tried. However, accurate data, however incomplete, would have provided a basis upon which to sort and process information that could have been used during the program and subsequently. For those displaced in incidents of violence that took place following the commencement of the UNDP program (between 1993 to 1995), UNDP could have been at the sites where the displaced were congregating to collect accurate data.

UNDP was the best placed organization to have collected the information on internally displaced numbers and needs, and the steps being taken meet these needs. The UNDP displaced persons program was the major and only national

---

Resolution 1995/56: Strengthening of the Coordination of Emergency Humanitarian Assistance," U.N. Doc. DP/1997/CRP.10, February 28, 1997, para. 18.

program in the country. It was the one actor with the capacity to access information from the widest range of sources, both inside and outside the government, and because of its stated partnership with the government, it was probably the organization that would have encountered the least government resistance. While much of the data that UNDP would have collected would have relied on the work of the local NGOs, none of these groups on their own could have undertaken the task as effectively. All of the local groups ran programs in certain areas, and while there was some cooperation, consultation, and even duplication, among the groups, there was no one local group well-placed to conduct anything on a national scale due to resource constraints and likely government obstruction. Often, numbers varied widely among the groups in part because of the difficulty of accurately registering the displaced, because of fraudulent or duplicate registrations, and even because of number inflation by some local groups themselves, perhaps for fund-raising purposes.

The regular collection and distribution of data on the situation of the internally displaced would have kept the spotlight on the Kenyan government. Had UNDP instituted a reporting procedure, which compiled and collated reports from its own staff and other sources, the program would have been better able to identify and register the displaced as well as to document what was happening to them in order to better follow their rehabilitation and reintegration. UNDP field officers were required to submit bi-weekly reports to UNDP; however, these reports were not regularly shared, even with donors. A diplomat who was based in Kenya at that time noted,

> This was indicative of the larger problem of their poor reporting. At the Excom meetings, UNDP, like many U.N. agencies, was very bad about reporting. They didn't give proper updates about what they were doing or what was happening. For instance, during the month of September [1994], they simply stated that they were busy with the Rogge visit.[142]

Findings about the situation should have been published at frequent intervals and in a manner that was accessible to those in Kenya as well as the international community. Regular public reporting by UNDP may have deterred abuses against the displaced by a government that was sensitive to negative publicity and its impact on renewed foreign aid.

---

[142]Human Rights Watch/Africa interview with diplomat formerly based in Kenya (name withheld on request), New York, July 12, 1996.

UNDP was not unaware that the lack of information on the displaced was a problem. In one of its earliest reports, UNDP noted that the numbers provided were inaccurate or too generalized and that data needed to be collected.[143] The first Rogge report recorded that:

> The numbers affected remain uncertain and somewhat speculative, as is invariably the case with internally displaced populations. Local government administrations have little or no substantive data on the numbers affected, past or present, or those currently in need of assistance. None have undertaken any systematic registration of displaced or otherwise affected persons. NGOs and church groups providing relief assistance to affected populations have made considerable effort to register their clients, but most concede that their numbers are only approximations. It is clear that there is some duplication in their registrations and that many non-affected persons succeed in getting themselves registered as beneficiaries. On the other hand, many displacees do not get registered at all because they have left affected regions to return to their ancestral lands to draw upon the assistance of relatives or friends. Others have simply "disappeared" into urban areas. Elsewhere, displacees who have returned, or are in [the] process of returning to their farms have remained outside the NGO assistance network and thus remain unenumerated.[144]

The lack of data also allowed for some duplicate or fraudulent claims for food relief and benefits by people claiming to be displaced. Conversely, lack of knowledge about assistance programs or fear of registering affected some, and they did not register at all. Either they left the area to live with relatives, were absorbed into the urban poor, or remained by choice outside of the food assistance network, thereby remaining uncounted.

Unfortunately, UNDP did not consider data collation a priority at all: not of the numbers of displaced that had occurred prior to their program, and not of those who were terrorized off their land in the midst of their program. Instead,

---

[143]Government of Kenya/UNDP, *Programme Document: Programme for Displaced Persons*, Inter-Agency Joint Programming, October 26, 1993, p.6-7.

[144]Rogge Report I, UNDP, September 1993, para.3.

UNDP relied on an approximation of 250,000,[145] which was the estimate given in the first Rogge report.[146] UNDP has stated:

> The estimates throughout were just that—estimates. This was made abundantly clear in both Rogge reports and UNDP had always indicated that the 250,000 figure that was being used was little more than a crude estimate. The number was, however, based exclusively on data provided to Rogge by the NGOs and Churches; at no time were any Government estimates used.[147]

UNDP then continued to use the same figure throughout, even though by its own count, large-scale violence in October 1993 in Enosupukia, Narok district, was known to have displaced 20,600 more people (7,090 adults and 13,551 children)[148] and in March 1994 in Burnt Forest another 10-12,000.[149] This should

---

[145]UNDP placed the number of displaced in April 1993 at 255,426. The breakdown of the figures by district was as follows: Bungoma, 21,100; Busia, 1,800; Elgon, 14,375; Kakamega, unknown; Vihiga, unknown; Kisumu, 8,975; Nyamira, 750; Kisii, 2,300; Kuria, unknown; Turkana, 16,625; Trans Nzoia, 18,525; Elgeyo-Marakwet, 22,300; Uasin Gishu, 82,000; Nandi, 17,850; Kericho, 6,550; Bomet, unknown; Narok, 900; Nakuru, 40,700; Laikipia, 600. John Rogge, "The Internal Displaced Population in Western, Nyanza and Rift Valley Provinces: A Needs Assessment and Rehabilitation Program," UNDP Draft Report as quoted in Government of Kenya/UNDP *Program Document: Program for Displaced Persons,* Inter-Agency Joint Programming, October 26, 1993, p.8.

[146]Many believe that this initial estimate was conservative, and that the estimate is more in the range of 300,000. See, for example, U.S. Committee for Refugees, *World Refugee Survey 1996* (Washington D.C.: Immigration and Refugee Services of America, 1996), p.53. When Human Rights Watch/Africa conducted research in 1993, it also estimated a total of 300,000 based on the finding that in many places the count of displaced persons cited included only the adults, ignoring the large numbers of displaced children (estimated by UNDP to make up some 75 percent of the total displaced population). Human Rights Watch/Africa, *Divide and Rule,* p.71.

[147]See Appendix: UNDP Response, pp.5-6.

[148]Summary report from the Enabling Environment Working Group contained in minutes of the second NCDP meeting, Methodist Guest House, Nairobi, November 1, 1994.

[149]Rogge Report II, UNDP, September 1994, 2.3.

have taken the estimated total up to 280,000, even by UNDP's count, which by its own admission errs on the cautious side. Yet, UNDP has continued to use the 250,000 figure up to today, which is at least 30,000 less than its estimated total should be.[150]

As the program unfolded, UNDP increasingly moved away from taking responsibility for collecting national data. The second Rogge report explicitly discouraged registration on the grounds that it created expectations and should therefore not be emphasized. Instead, Rogge urged that the program should focus on areas or zones where people were still displaced on the grounds that there was little to gain from obtaining exact numbers.[151] To the contrary, the purpose of

---

[150]UNDP's response is twofold: (1) "The specific response to the Rogge report underestimating numbers by 30,000 was explained at a meeting with the HRW [Human Rights Watch] in New York in February. This explanation has not been taken into consideration in the current report. The issue concerned data for Mt. Elgon region where the NCCK [National Council of Churches] had greatly inflated numbers. Rogge opted on the side of caution to adjust these numbers to what he saw on the ground. He was subsequently proved right in doing this since two months after the survey, the NCCK Relief Co-ordinator for the Mt. Elgon area was removed for misappropriating relief funds and was accused of greatly inflating the number of beneficiaries in his area. The missing 30,000 to which the HRW refers in report are the 30,000 which the NCCK Co-ordinator was accused of inflating" and (2) "A more basic issue is that given the uncertainties of the data, to dwell extensively on whether the numbers were 250,000 or 280,000 is somewhat irrelevant." See Appendix: UNDP Response, p.6.

Human Rights Watch met in January 1995 (not February), with Resident Representative to Kenya, David Whaley, and Senior Technical Advisor, Killian Kleinschmidt. The interview notes of that meeting, however, indicate no reference to UNDP taking into account number inflation in Mt. Elgon. With regard to the second response, Human Rights Watch/Africa agrees that extensive dwelling on the exact number serves little purpose. However, UNDP has been accused by the NGO community of underestimating the total displaced and inflating the numbers reintegrated. The Kenyan government has also capitalized on the lack of accurate data to evade its responsibilities to the displaced. In such a situation, an explanation of the numbers is warranted.

[151]The report read: "It is suggested that less emphasis be placed on further systematic registrations of affected populations by concerned NGOs and religious institutions. Registrations of individuals always create expectations, and expectations invariably produce more 'beneficiaries.' As relief interventions are replaced by rehabilitation and reconstruction inputs, it makes much more sense to now focus on clearly identifying and targeting areas/communities which have been affected by the disturbances or into which displacees have settled or are returning. The rapid transition from targeting

collating and documenting the names of those displaced would have provided a basis upon which to identify those scattered or converted into urban slum dwellers. A UNDP official told Human Rights Watch/Africa:

> In retrospect, we should have paid more attention to registering the displaced. But we did what we thought was best at the time. It seemed that there were more pressing things to deal with and we thought, at that time, by taking this approach we could achieve more.[152]

Realizing that a lack of data or information on the whereabouts of the displaced would not only dissipate national and international outrage over the situation but also permanently subvert reintegration efforts, the government systematically dispersed congregations of displaced, which were easily visible to journalists, human rights and relief workers. The government capitalized on the lack of such data by scattering congregations of displaced, using threats, intimidation, and in some cases force, making it impossible to assess the current situation or locate those who remain off their land. For example, in late December 1994, the government told clash victims at the Eldoret NCCK community center to move back to their farms. The Uasin Gishu DO, Daniel Lotoai, also made it clear that the government would only aid clash victims on their farms and not in centers and camps.[153] Another example is the dispersal and relocation of thousands at Maela camp when the government left them at several random sites in Central Province without food or shelter. The lack of data by UNDP made the government's job all the easier since dispersed populations, while not reintegrated, were no longer identifiable. Many have become an urban working class and have disappeared into the anonymity of the cities and towns.

---

resources at individuals to targeting them at communities will also significantly accelerate the process of reconciliation." Rogge Report II, UNDP, September 1994, Executive Summary, para.9; and presentation by John Rogge, UNDP consultant contained in minutes of the third Excom Meeting, Kenyatta International Conference Centre, Nairobi, September 8, 1994.

[152]Human Rights Watch/Africa interview with UNDP official (name withheld on request), New York, February 26, 1997.

[153]"Internal Refugee Families Ordered to Leave Eldoret," KNA News Agency: Nairobi, in English 1444 gmt, December 28, 1994.

The lack of accurate data has also been questionably used by UNDP to put the best face on its program in Kenya. UNDP has been consistently accused of downplaying the total number of displaced, while inflating its estimates of those reintegrated. UNDP's first attempt at estimating the numbers of those who had gone home was after the program had been in existence for one year. In the second Rogge report of September 1994, UNDP consultant John Rogge stated:

> [f]or the whole of western Kenya, an optimistic estimate might be that one third of the affected population is now back on its land and in the process of rebuilding its houses...A much larger proportion, perhaps as much as half of the total displaced in western Kenya, are in a transitional state of return.[154]

The wording was repeated by former UNDP resident representative to Kenya, David Whaley, at a NCDP meeting. This assertion was then given the highest stamp of authority by UNDP when Administrator James Gustave Speth, on a visit to Kenya in September 1994, held a news conference publicly and definitively stating that "thirty percent of the 250,000 clash victims have been rehabilitated, 50 percent have moved closer to their shambas [farms in Kiswahili], while there are intricate land disputes involving the rest."[155] At a dinner hosted for him by the government, Mr. Speth noted that he was impressed by the government's efforts to restore peace and rehabilitate the displacees, stating that "in a world of ethnic strife, what we saw during the visit to Molo is a government which is moving to reconcile tribal differences."[156] Mr. Speth made no mention of the continued threats or actual violence against the displaced, forced dispersals, the destruction of camp sites by administration police, or government harassment of those assisting the displaced.[157] Mr. Speth also stated that Kenya would always be

---

[154]Rogge Report II, UNDP, September 1994, p.2(4)(5).

[155]"75,000 Clashes' Victims Resettled," *Daily Nation* (Nairobi), September 14, 1994.

[156]"A Little More Respect for the Truth, Please," *The Weekly Review* (Nairobi), September 23, 1994.

[157]UNDP takes issue with Human Rights Watch/Africa's assessment that Mr. Speth did not hint at human rights problems which needed to be addressed. UNDP points out that Mr. Speth "clearly made the point that while as many as one-third of the displaced

a friend of UNDP and that UNDP would continue to call for increased assistance to Kenya.[158]

According to UNDP, the 1994 estimate of those reintegrated was reached:

> based on what the NGOs on the ground reported, including the Peace and Justice Commission [*sic*] in Nakuru. The proposal in the Rogge report clearly stated that perhaps as much as a third were back living on their land and about half of the total were cultivating their land but not necessarily living on it, i.e. the other half were displaced. John Rogge presented these "numbers" to an NGO seminar on the displaced shortly before his departure and the NGOs present did not disagree with the validity of these assertions. Hence, the U.N. team used these numbers as working estimates for the programme.[159]

However, the assertion by UNDP that its program had resettled approximately one third of the displaced created an uproar among local relief and church organizations. UNDP's estimates of those who remained displaced was 30 percent fewer than the 240,000 estimated by the local relief organizations.[160] Advocates for the displaced charged UNDP and the government of understating the number of people who remained uprooted.

When called on to offer proof of this figure, UNDP quickly sought to distance itself from its own estimate of those reintegrated. Not unlike the Kenyan government, which constantly blames others (including the press) for the ethnic violence, UNDP disingenuously accused the Kenyan press —which had cited a figure of 75,000 by calculating one third of UNDP's estimated total of 250,000—of manipulating the figure and taking it out of context. UNDP claimed that it had

---

persons had been resettled, there remained many who remained displaced...[and] there were still intricate land disputes involving the rest." See Appendix: UNDP Response, p.4.

[158]"U.N. Body Reassures Kenya on Support," *Daily Nation* (Nairobi), September 13, 1994.

[159]See Appendix: UNDP Response, pp.3-4.

[160]U.S. Committee for Refugees, *1995 World Survey Report* (Washington D.C.: Immigration and Refugee Services of America, 1995), p.62.

never used that numerical figure (which is technically correct, since it had used the wording one third).[161]

In late 1995, when UNDP ended its displaced persons program, it announced that some 180,000 persons had been resettled as a result of the program. While Human Rights Watch/Africa is not in the position to verify the exact number of displaced remaining at this time, it does appear from interviews with local and international relief workers who were, and still are, assisting the displaced that the UNDP estimate is greatly inflated. David Round-Turner, former policy advisor with the UNDP program, is also of the opinion that the figures are high. He said, "UNDP was counting as returned even those who were staying at market centers, but who were returning to cultivate their land during the day. If you do that, you get a much larger figure of returnees."[162] Ernest Murimi of the Catholic Justice and Peace Commission flatly refuted UNDP's estimate that its program has reintegrated some 180,000:

> That figure surprised us. People in the field were not consulted about that figure. Where did it come from? The government? We asked UNDP to give us the names of the people who have been resettled here, we were told to ask the D.C. [District Commissioner]. UNDP should have—as its first priority—created a reliable registration system. Now it is too late. UNDP failed miserably. Where did they resettle people? Where is their evaluation? These numbers they put out—ask them where they got them from. Where is the list of names? Which regions are they from? We [the Justice and Peace Commission] can show you our list of people. Where they came

---

[161]Killian Kleinschmidt, Senior Technical Advisor, UNDP Displaced Persons Program, "The Programme for Displaced Persons and Communities Affected by the Ethnic Violence in Kenya," UNDP, November 1994, p.2; and NCCK, "UNDP Official Disputes Resettlement Story," *Clashes Update*, (Nairobi: NCCK), no.21, October 27, 1994, pp.1-2.

[162]Human Rights Watch/Africa interview with David Round-Turner, former Policy Advisor, UNDP Displaced Persons Program, Nairobi, August 26, 1996.

from, where they are, if they are back on their land. UNDP has not been transparent.[163]

One diplomat said:

> Even if UNDP wanted to come in today and rectify the damage it was party to, it would be impossible to locate all the displaced because of the lack of documentation. UNDP never even followed up on those who were forcibly removed from Maela camp. They didn't even take on the responsibility of retrieving those people who were transported in lorries with fuel that UNDP paid for and were left by the side of the road in Central Province. Who knows where these people are now? Certainly not UNDP, and maybe no one.[164]

Had UNDP created a national database to register the displaced and to document the site of their displacement, the possibility of assisting those who remain displaced today would have been greatly augmented.

Reluctance to Criticize the Government's Human Rights Abuses

"UNDP has done a magnificent job in Kenya"
—President Daniel arap Moi, September 1994

A major criticism leveled at UNDP was its unwillingness to speak out against the Kenyan government's past and continuing role in intimidating, harassing, and even terrorizing the internally displaced. While UNDP certainly can not be held responsible for the recalcitrant behavior of the Kenyan government, it can, be held responsible for not structuring the program in such a way to place safeguards against human rights violations; for not taking a lead role in speaking out against ongoing rights violations; and for not assisting the displaced to redress past and existing wrongs. There were a wide variety of human rights issues that

---

[163]Human Rights Watch/Africa interview with Earnest Murimi, Executive Secretary, Justice and Peace Commission, Catholic Diocese of Nakuru, Nakuru, August 6, 1996.

[164]Human Rights Watch/Africa interview with a diplomat (name withheld on request), Nairobi, July 30, 1996.

UNDP should have monitored. Among the issues that needed to be addressed were the denial of basic human rights to the displaced; the harassment, intimidation and forced dispersals of the displaced; the complete lack of accountability for the perpetrators and inciters of the violence; and the expropriation and arbitrary tampering with legal titles to formally disinherit them of the land owned by the displaced. Instead, UNDP's silence on these issues gave the misleading impression that all was going well with the program and eventually undermined and compromised the reintegration process.

According to UNDP, it constantly raised human rights issues with senior government officials in private meetings.[165] Quiet representations by UNDP were fine. However, when the Kenyan government continued to ignore such representations, it was incumbent on UNDP to become more outspoken about what was happening as well as to distance itself from the government in a manner that was apparent to Kenyans and the international community. UNDP's approach suited the Kenyan government. It allowed them to continue to pursue their policy of ethnic persecution and prevention of return to select areas of land, certain in the knowledge that UNDP was not going to be publicly critical in such a way that would require the government to reverse the damage it had done. In fact, UNDP did more than just remain silent in the face of continuing abuses. Its public statements about the Kenyan government and the program, particularly during the September 1994 visit of Administrator James Gustave Speth,[166] heaped praise on

---

[165]UNDP also says that it constantly raised these concerns publicly, and that its unflinching criticism of human rights violations was eventually the element that brought the joint program to a halt. Appendix: UNDP Response, p.4.

This statement is not wholly accurate. Human Rights Watch/Africa has examined virtually every public statement and UNDP document on this program. UNDP only became vocal in December 1994-January 1995 after the forced dispersals at Maela. Prior to that, its handful of references to human rights violations minimized them as the individual actions of a few government officials. The UNDP program did not come to a halt because UNDP spoke up about ethnic discrimination and forced expulsions. The UNDP program ended because it had never been structured in such a way as to incorporate safeguards and mechanisms, as a pre-condition of the program, that would have made it more difficult for the government pursue its policies of ethnic persecution.

[166]Indicative of the appearance of complicity between UNDP and the Kenya government was an editorial piece contained in the government-owned *Kenya Times* newspaper which stated: "Mr. Speth cocked a snook at Kenya's ill-informed critics, domestic and foreign, when he expressed complete satisfaction with the resettlement of families displaced during ethnic clashes in Molo and the efforts being made by the

the government, leaving the misleading impression that it was only a matter of time before everyone would go home. The perceived indifference to human rights abuses that UNDP demonstrated ultimately was detrimental to the long-term prospects of all the displaced and allowed the government to use UNDP as a cover for ongoing abuse.

Some of the reasons the UNDP program in Kenya appeared unprepared or unwilling to deal with this inevitable and integral aspect of working with some displaced populations are discussed below. However, regardless of the reasons, the result was that human rights monitoring and advocacy were not a prominent component of the program. There was no effort by UNDP to sensitize its staff and that of the Kenyan government working on the program to human rights standards and policies relating to the internally displaced. There was also no effort to document, report, or publicize the violations against the displaced; to mobilize international attention to the situation of the displaced; or, when necessary, to shame the government into complying with the reintegration process. While there was talk by UNDP of the need for the government to create an enabling environment, no effort was made to promulgate articulated standards and to make these the minimum conditions for going forward with the displaced program. Instead of pressing the Kenyan government to adopt policies that would have created an enabling environment, UNDP officials avoided any denunciation of the abuses.

In large part, UNDP's silence can be explained by the fact that it does not have a history of addressing the situations it is now dealing with in emergency programs. While it has commendably grown to deal with the changing world, some of its working practices have not as of yet adapted. UNDP as an institution has traditionally worked closely with government partners. Some surmise that UNDP's decision to align itself closely with the Kenyan government was an

---

Government to bring about reconciliation among the so-called rival communities. 'In a world of ethnic strife, what we saw during the visit to Molo is a Government, which is moving to reconcile tribal differences,' he said, and expressed the hope that Kenya would lead the way in ethnic reconciliation just as it had done in sustainable development. This, indeed, is a heartening and well-deserved compliment from a well-informed person of Mr. Speth's stature. On Monday, President Moi lauded the work being done by UNDP when Mr. Speth called on him at State House, Nairobi. The Head of State said that the UNDP had done a magnificent job in Kenya...We on our part are grateful to Mr. Speth for his clear-headed vision of Kenya as a leading nation in Africa and to UNDP for pledging $80 million for various projects in the country. We hope that Mr. Speth will see to it that his organization releases much more financial assistance for Kenya as early as possible." "UNDP Official's Views Encouraging." *Kenya Times* (Nairobi), September 14, 1994.

intentional policy decision as with all other programs it runs. Further, UNDP has traditionally not perceived its role as an advocate on human rights protection. In the face of government abuse, its institutional instinct is not to address human rights and protection issues, as some other U.N. agencies such as UNHCR, for example, would have been more inclined to do. UNDP officials justified their public silence to Human Rights Watch/Africa in a meeting in January 1995 as the price paid to secure various operational goals that would ultimately help the displaced.[167]

As a result of its background, UNDP did not have extensive staff experience in this area. Human rights experience and expertise at the field level on how best to approach these difficult issues appeared to be lacking. As a result, instead of addressing government actions detrimental to the situation of the displaced, abusive actions on the part of the government were often explained away by UNDP field staff in a manner that mitigated government responsibility and accountability. For example, UNDP officials on the Kenya program were quick to make excuses for the president's inaction, dismissing setbacks in the program as the individual actions of certain government officials who were beyond his control, such as Rift Valley P.C. Ismael Chelanga or Ministers Nicholas Biwott and William Ntimama, who continued to make inflammatory statements against the displaced. While the assessment by UNDP that identifiable individuals within the government were responsible for inciting the clashes is correct, the conclusion that President Moi and the state as a whole was not in control and therefore could not be held responsible incorrectly removed the responsibility of the government to act. Ultimate responsibility for reintegrating the displaced remains with President Moi and his government, whether individuals in the government are inciting the violence independently or not.

UNDP officials also sought to downplay the political nature of the ethnic violence, portraying it as if it was some complex, inscrutable problem of Africa that foreigners could never understand. Additionally, there was an attempt to downplay the fact that there were victims and aggressors and to portray the problem as one of shattered communities, ignoring the justice and accountability issues involved for those affected by the violence, be they Kikuyu, Luo, Luhya or Kalenjin.[168]

---

[167]Human Rights Watch/Africa interview with David Whaley, former UNDP Resident Representative to Kenya and Killian Kleinschmidt, former UNDP Senior Technical Advisor to the Displaced Persons Program, New York, January 12, 1995.

[168]Human Rights Watch/Africa interviews with UNDP officials, local and international NGOs, journalists and academics between 1993 and 1997.

It was also widely perceived that the UNDP silence around government actions was because UNDP officials tended to negatively equate any criticism of government policies as being supportive of the political opposition, which it sought to distance itself from. Some have chalked this up to the conclusion that the UNDP resident representative at the time did believe that the government was making a good faith effort, due to his consistent public position in defense of the government's record. An academic who interviewed UNDP officials in the course of conducting research on Kenya had this observation to make about the UNDP program:

> My sense of it, broadly speaking, is that UNDP accepted, or were trapped in, a situation affording limited autonomy—perhaps even no autonomy whatsoever. What autonomy they had seemed to be defined as intermediaries between the "two sides" meaning the government of Kenya (or Kalenjin) versus the opposition (Kikuyu). Both sides were seen as equally culpable, but they had a stronger link to the government, given that it was their program partner. Their relations with the other side, the opposition, were weak, and suspicion was the norm. In our interviews they were concerned, I think, to convince us that the opposition was a major, if not the major, problem. They also seemed to see themselves as almost co-rulers.[169]

Another explanation for UNDP's silence on human rights issues at the field level—and its deflection of criticism of Kenya's record—has been attributed to the institutional structure at UNDP which does not encourage or promote staff initiative in protecting human rights. First, the dual designation of resident representative and resident coordinators poses problems. UNDP resident representatives are expected, as a requirement of their job, to foster close working relations with the host government. That same person is then designated resident coordinator to lead an emergency program, such as a displaced persons program, that may require criticism of government policy. This dual designation poses inherent tensions for the resident representative. In the Kenyan situation, this tension certainly was present. One UNDP official said:

---

[169]Human Rights Watch/Africa interview with Professor Frank Holmquist, Hampshire College, Amherst, January 16, 1997.

David Whaley [former UNDP Resident Representative to Kenya] came close to being made *persona non grata* and losing a promotion because he stuck his neck out on the displaced persons program in Kenya. Moreover, he did not get the backing of New York to address some of the key issues, such as legal reforms on land tenure. Sometimes the people in the field feel that they are not getting the support they need from headquarters. When they want to take a certain direction or speak up, they are stopped from doing so by people in headquarters who are not as well informed about what is happening or who reinforce the agency's tradition of good relations with the government.[170]

Second, there is no formal human rights reporting requirement by UNDP headquarters. This further reinforced the silence on human rights violations in the Displaced Persons Program in Kenya. Regular situation reports, which documented the situation including human rights violations, were a required part of the work of the UNDP field officers. However, these reports remained cursory and did not serve to increase international attention to the human rights situation of the displaced. One internal donor report assessing the UNDP program in 1994 stated:

The information flow was never as forthcoming as it should have been. For example, though field officers were asked to submit bi-weekly reports, these were not shared with donors. This is part of the larger global problem of [UNDP's] poor reporting. Though lack of capacity is repeatedly cited, it seems to go beyond that to a reluctance to share the problems as well as the success stories.[171]

This approach was detrimental to the implementation of the program on the ground. UNDP did not put into place safeguards to avoid government manipulation of the program nor did it create mechanisms to monitor and protect

---

[170]Human Rights Watch/Africa interview with UNDP official (name withheld on request), New York, February 26, 1997.

[171]Internal donor evaluation of the UNDP program (donor name withheld on request) November 1994, provided to Human Rights Watch/Africa, July 1996.

the displaced from government actions. A former UNDP employee who worked on the program said "UNDP made a political miscalculation about the Kenyan government's intentions in agreeing to this program." He said:

> UNDP started well, but quickly the program was almost a total failure. The problems came when it let the government come in strongly. The government channeled UNDP funds through the ministries of education, health and agriculture. The local D.C.s were allowed to chair the committees. They overruled the local input. The D.O.s were signatories to the accounts. They signed the checks. Through the local administration, and out of sight of the international and national groups based in Nairobi, the national government exercised extensive control over the UNDP program.[172]

An international humanitarian worker said:

> Throughout, we were frustrated that UNDP did not play a role in addressing the political issues. We thought that we would address the relief and medical emergency needs and that their role would be to find lasting solutions to get people home—hard agreements with the government. David Whaley [former UNDP resident representative to Kenya] and Philippe Chichereau [former UNDP senior technical advisor] talked like they believed they had something with the government, and each time the government undermined the program they acted surprised. After a while, we gave up expecting anything from UNDP.[173]

Any prospect of UNDP support for accountability for past abuses was a further casualty of the reluctance to grapple with the political issues that might jeopardize a close partnership. There was a deliberate decision not to pass judgment on the actual clashes on the grounds that it was up to Kenyan society, not outsiders, to determine the manner in which it would deal with the tragic elements

---

[172]Human Rights Watch/Africa interview with former UNDP Displaced Persons Program employee (name withheld on request), Nakuru, August 7, 1996.

[173]Human Rights Watch/Africa interview with international relief worker (name withheld on request), Nairobi, July 30, 1996.

of its past. However, where serious human rights abuses form the backdrop to a humanitarian crisis, the U.N. should not operate its programs as if it were writing on a blank slate. Unaddressed rights and justice issues of the past inevitably come back to haunt prospects for lasting reconciliation and peace. The U.N. programs for the internally displaced must incorporate a mechanism that can be used to address abuses that have occurred, including the prosecution of offenders in the national courts. There was also concern that UNDP involvement would allow government officials to portray the situation as a mere "development" problem and allow the government to underplay its damaging political role in fomenting and exacerbating the violence; let alone in consolidating the displacement through expropriations and underhanded land title switches.

Human rights documentation and regular reporting should have been one of the primary means to begin to halt abuses and prevent them from worsening. In this sense, UNDP could have served as an international witness to violations and been the primary force behind mobilizing the appropriate protection measures. Regular public reporting would have helped to ensure that human rights concerns were not subordinated to other political considerations and should have been a component of the UNDP program. It should have been required to publish updates at frequent intervals in a manner accessible to both Kenyans and the international community.

In order to implement emergency-type programs, such as displaced persons programs, where human rights violations are often central to the success of the program, UNDP must evolve and expand the perception of its traditional role at the implementation level to incorporate human rights advocacy and protection work. Internal displacement, by its nature, frequently has human rights concerns at its core and the agency must be prepared to stand up to government abuses. Where private entreaties with the government do not work, UNDP must be prepared to use more public means or mobilize pressure from other quarters. Inevitably, that will introduce some discord with government officials. However, that must be the minimum price for respect for fundamental rights.

No Protection Component

"UNDP did not speak out when we needed protection from the government."
—Kikuyu displaced person, Maela, Nakuru District, August 7, 1996

Protection and security have not been central concerns for many humanitarian and development agencies involved with the internally displaced. Protection of the physical safety and the human rights of the internally displaced must be as much a part of international programs as the provision of relief assistance, because security threats often undermine the ability for the displaced to return to their land. Protection is a clearly established concept within the refugee protection framework and the responsibilities of UNHCR. However, since it is often U.N. agencies other than UNHCR that are administering programs for the internally displaced, the result is that a strong protection component is frequently lacking. UNDP was no exception in this regard. UNDP, as a routine matter, does not include or view protection concerns as part of its traditional mandate. Few staff on programs for the internally displaced have expertise to deal with the physical safety of the displaced, even in places where protection issues are paramount. However, programs that deal with the internally displaced are made more difficult by the security and political issues surrounding the nature of their displacement than many other development projects in which UNDP is involved in worldwide.[174]

Protection issues with the displaced in Kenya came up both with regard to ensuring physical security from threats of coercion and violence, and the longer term issues of defending legal rights that were violated by those responsible for the displacement. Within the ambit of protection activities, UNDP should have also seen its role as providing an umbrella of protection to the local and international relief organizations working with the displaced. Yet, there was some resistance within UNDP to interpreting its mandate to include protection responsibilities on the grounds that it would be too "political" and would jeopardize the ability of the agency to provide relief assistance. However, without a protection component, programs for the internally displaced will be prone to serious setbacks.

UNDP itself knew this, but ultimately did not do anything about it. The first Rogge report clearly stated:

> The question of security throughout the clash areas is fundamental to the success of any rehabilitation and reconstruction program. This can only be provided through a forceful and sustained commitment by the highest echelons of the Government of Kenya and all its responsible local administrations, including local chiefs and elected local councillors. Local agitation by any party against any ethnic group must be immediately and forcefully aborted at its source. Perpetrators of violence such as looting must be dealt with as

---

[174]See Roberta Cohen, "Protecting the Internally Displaced," *World Refugee Survey 1996*, (U.S. Committee for Refugees, Washington D.C.: Immigration and Refugee Services of America, 1996), p.23.

common criminals and brought expeditiously before the full process of the law.[175]

In a mission report written two years later, UNDP once again underscored the need for protection:

> The role played by Government in providing security to all citizens is paramount. There can be no half measures. Amid all the needs expressed by those displaced or affected by clashes, security is predominant: physical security, of person and property; security to plant and harvest crops; security of title, of lease and the security to carry on legitimate business regardless of ethnicity.[176]

Although the provision of security is ultimately the responsibility of the government, UNDP had a major role to play in making the Kenyan government commit to provide the necessary security for the displaced to return to their land. Since 1993 until the present, many of the displaced interviewed by Human Rights Watch/Africa expressed a willingness to return to their land, provided there was adequate security. Security does not necessarily mean a heightened police presence in an area (particularly where the police were previously shown to take sides in the violence), but rather a genuine reassurance and tangible steps by the national government to engender confidence among the displaced that the government will not tolerate any intimidation or violence and that prompt government action will be taken to avert violence.

It was critical that UNDP insist that the Kenyan government ensure adequate security for the program, facilitate access to areas and send a clear message throughout its administration for transparency and efficiency. Repeated calls from donors for the Kenyan government to step up this role continued during the UNDP program.[177] The threat of insecurity—real or perceived—remains up to today a major impediment to return. From the outset, UNDP should have worked

---

[175]Rogge Report I, UNDP, September 1993, para. 8.

[176]UNDP, "UNDP Mission Report," April 18-22, 1995, p.4.

[177]British High Commissioner Sir Kieran Prendergast called on the government to do this at the second NCDP meeting. Minutes of the second NCDP meeting, Methodist Guest House, Nairobi, November 1, 1994.

immediately with the security forces and local administration, providing training on rights and legal responsibilities to create a vision of what their role should be in the reintegration process. Similar efforts conducted by UNHCR with Kenyan police in Northeastern Province have resulted in a notable difference in diminishing police abuses against the refugee population in the area and enhanced security for the refugees from outside attackers (see section on Strengthening the U.N. Framework to Protect the Displaced).

UNDP must develop clearer protection politics for its programs for the internally displaced, which center around protecting lives and safety, defending legal and human rights and promoting international standards. UNDP should have, as an absolute prerequisite of the program, insisted on minimum protection safeguards.

Strained Relations with Donors

Donor governments can often play a role in raising human rights violations and other concerns with governments. In situations where the U.N. is better served by not publicly speaking out on an issue, often donor governments can step in to raise issues on behalf of the U.N. For UNDP in Kenya, the donor voice could have provided the opportunity to raise the more controversial issues that UNDP felt constrained to raise. Yet, Human Rights Watch/Africa interviews with donors and UNDP officials on the Kenyan program often degenerated into a finger-pointing exercise. Officials in UNDP expressed the belief that the some donors, who had originally asked for the Kenya program, ultimately did not provide the necessary funding to make it succeed, and some donors, in turn, accused UNDP of not informing or mobilizing the donors to address the problems in the program.

The donors in Kenya represented a potentially powerful ally in raising human rights issues. The Moi government, although often publicly hostile to donor influence, has had a long history of responding to donor pressure with regard to human rights and economic reform. Through such sustained donor pressure, some significant human rights gains have been obtained in Kenya including the government's abandonment of the use of the Preservation of Public Security Act to detain critics indefinitely without charge, the restoration of tenure to judges as well as relative improvements in freedoms of expression, assembly and association. Although the situation in Kenya today is by no means ideal, there has been a relative improvement in the rights situation since the mid-1980s, in large part due to multilateral and bilateral donor pressure that augmented the domestic calls for change. This is not to say that human rights and protection issues were the sole determining factor in decisions on aid and investment, nor that the donors could have been relied on give this issue priority over other national interests. However, the donors did take an interest in the situation of the displaced in Kenya, and themselves expressed concern about the government's actions against the displaced.

UNDP had ready access to the donor community through its Executive Committee (Excom) of the National Committee for Displaced Persons (NCDP). Excom was made up of two members each from the government, bilateral donors, multilateral donors, religious organizations and NGOs. One of the terms of reference of the Excom was to "Discuss and develop approach, policy and strategy of the long term programme on the basis of the Rogge report, its recommendations and subsequent reports." The Excom provided a useful structure through which donors were able to provide feedback to the government about the progress.

UNDP did use the NCDP and other mechanisms to keep donors informed. During the preparatory phase, the resident representative had regular briefings with donor representatives and the Rogge report was made available to all. However, according to donor representatives, UNDP could have taken far better advantage of the presence of the donor countries in Excom, which included representatives from Kenya's major donors—including the U.S., the U.K and the E.U.—to put pressure on the Kenyan government where UNDP for whatever reason did not want to. However, some donors noted that UNDP did not fully inform or engage their embassies and that UNDP was not always responsive in terms of answering to the members of Excom, as they were theoretically supposed to be. One diplomat formerly based in Kenya said, "They [The UNDP Displaced Persons Program] seemed to respond to the upper echelons of UNDP. They needed to be held more accountable to the Excom. UNDP would often go off and do its own thing and then call in other parties when they needed to hide behind the curtain of 'Excom.'"[178]

One explanation offered by one UNDP official who had worked on the program was that UNDP was in a dilemma because it was simultaneously seeking funding from the same donor countries and, had the program been portrayed as problematic, it might have lost funding prospects that it was already having a difficult time obtaining. However, UNDP's perceived silence about the human rights problems in the program had its own detrimental effect on the way donors perceived the program. Some NCDP members became wary of being too close to the UNDP program and became progressively less inclined to commit funding because of UNDP's unwillingness to speak out against government abuses or to

---

[178]Human Rights Watch/Africa interview with diplomat formerly based in Kenya (name withheld on request), New York, July 12, 1996.

mobilize the donor community. To some donors, UNDP's response to the forced dispersals at Maela confirmed these reservations. Following the dispersals, a meeting of the Excom was called to discuss the events at Maela. The government refused to attend: neither of the two Kenyan government officials involved with the UNDP program, Wilfred Kimilat from the Office of the President and Excom chair Paul Langat, made themselves available for the meeting, suggesting alternative dates. Yet David Whaley, UNDP Resident Representative to Kenya at the time, continued to try to accommodate and excuse the government's actions as something less than what they were. The January 4, 1995, meeting that was held without a government presence was termed an "informal meeting" for purposes of information exchange in order to placate a possible negative government reaction if a formal Excom meeting was held. It was at that meeting that David Whaley characterized the forced dispersal of thousands of Maela residents as a "temporary hiccup" in the program, further reinforcing donor scepticism about UNDP. A diplomat who attended the Excom meetings said:

> Donors never believed that the government was serious about this program. We also never had a sense that UNDP was willing to rock the boat. They were too cautious. In front of us, David Whaley said the right words, but frankly, the necessary action was missing. As a result, we were unwilling to make a large financial commitment to this program because we didn't have confidence in the Kenyan government or UNDP's willingness to push the government where it needed to be pushed."[179]

UNDP should have demanded more involvement from the donor governments on the Excom. This group of donors has traditionally been very influential in changing Kenyan government policy through lobbying. A strong coalition of bilateral donors could have strengthened UNDP's position and also allowed UNDP to raise concerns strongly without doing so itself.

---

[179]Human Rights Watch/Africa interview with a diplomat (name withheld on request), Nairobi, August 8, 1996.

Undermining Local Nongovernmental Efforts

"UNDP needed to work as a partner with the groups on the ground, not as a bulldozer."
—*Local NGO worker, Namwele, Bungoma district, August 3, 1996*

A potential strength of the U.N. in working with internally displaced populations is the capacity to back up and strengthen local partners in the task of assisting and protecting the displaced. NGOs have developed a wealth of experience, probably more so than the U.N., in dealing with displaced populations. The local NGOs are often closer to the ground and have better links and a more thorough grasp of the situation. Local groups also remain longer than international programs, and therefore strengthening national institutions and grassroots efforts can in turn strengthen the ability of this civil society sector successfully to demand government accountability. Conversely, the weakening of the NGO sector allows greater unchecked opportunities for government abuse of power.

By the time UNDP became involved with the displaced, almost two years after the clashes began, the local NGOs, particularly the NCCK and the Catholic Church, had been (and remain today) the primary providers of emergency relief and assistance to the displaced. In some areas, the local groups had begun cooperating and sometimes organized joint relief committees to coordinate the assistance. These local organizations had several main advantages over UNDP at the outset in that they had close proximity to the displaced and had functional structures in the displaced areas. More importantly, they had developed the trust of the victims. In turn, UNDP could have played a useful role in mitigating some of the less admirable practices of certain NGOs, including duplication of effort, inflation of numbers for fund-raising purposes, corruption, and a stress on charity and food aid rather than reintegration or long-term activities. In fact, the second Rogge report raised the latter problem.

When the UNDP program began, its stated plans broadly included provisions to work with and assist nongovernmental and church organizations. Yet, without exception, all the local NGOs and church organizations interviewed by Human Rights Watch/Africa accuse UNDP of distancing itself from the local groups that had been working with the displaced, and in some cases even of undermining and inadvertently destroying local efforts. Without exception, the Kenyan NGOs interviewed by Human Rights Watch/Africa believe that the relationship with UNDP was, as one NGO worker put it, "a one-way street." It is a widely shared view among the NGOs that UNDP took credit for their successes but did not strengthen their programs or defend them from government criticism for the work they were doing. One 1994 internal donor assessment of the UNDP program noted:

> UNDP does not have the universal respect of NGOs on the ground. Because of the close nature of their work with the GOK [government of Kenya], they are often perceived as being an instrument of the GOK. Further, in at least one district, cultural insensitivity [on the part] of a UNDP field officer has resulted in the alienation of other NGO groups and the District Officer.[180]

Some attribute this to the fact that the NGOs and churches were not only providing relief assistance to the displaced, but they were also speaking out about the government's role in fomenting the violence and harassing the displaced. As a result, these groups had come under strong attack from the government, which accused them of everything from sedition to treason. Others chalk it up to UNDP's decision to partner itself so closely to the government that it had to distance itself from the NGOs to avoid similar accusations. Ernest Murimi of the Catholic Justice and Peace Commission noted: "UNDP should have tapped into existing structures that the NGO community in Kenya had already set up. Instead, they came in and centralized their program through the local government administration structures and completely marginalized the NGOs."[181]

The one area that is repeatedly cited by UNDP as its success story of reintegration— and by the NGOs as a prime example of UNDP's damaging effect on local NGO reintegration efforts—is in Western Province. When UNDP came in to Western Province, it centralized all efforts in the area through the Western Province Coordinating Committee (WPCC), replacing a similar body which had been previously set up by the local NGOs. Tecla Wanjala, who worked with an NGO in the area at that time said:

> The groundwork for the resettlement had already been done by the time UNDP came. We were doing it before UNDP. We had formed a coordinating committee with the local groups—Action

---

[180]Internal donor evaluation of the UNDP program (donor name withheld on request), November 1994, provided to Human Rights Watch/Africa, July 1996.

[181]Human Rights Watch/Africa interview, Ernest Murimi with Executive Secretary, Justice and Peace Commission, Catholic Diocese of Nakuru, Nakuru, August 6, 1996.

Aid, the Kenya Red Cross, the Catholic Church, the Church
Province of Kenya and the NCCK. We struggled to get our
programs coordinated to better serve the area. By the time
UNDP took over the WPCC in 1994, we had even employed a
coordinator. Then UNDP came in and hijacked the process.
They didn't want to work closely with us, the local NGOs,
because the government was attacking us for helping the
displaced. Instead, they hijacked our structures and distanced
themselves from us. All donor funding began to go to UNDP
and therefore all projects began to get funding through UNDP.
Then, without notice, after Maela, UNDP withdrew and closed
down its program in 1995. Now, the momentum that the local
organizations had created is gone, and UNDP is gone, and we
have no way financially to sustain the efforts that we had begun
before UNDP came. So, the local efforts have collapsed. Now
there is a complete vacuum.[182]

The Centre for Refugee Studies at Moi University, Eldoret, was
commissioned by UNDP to assess independently UNDP's role in Western
Province, the one area which UNDP touted as its success story for fund-raising
purposes. When UNDP received a negative assessment of its role in the area, the
reported response of UNDP official William Lorenz, who received the staff of the
Centre for Refugee Studies, can only be described as hostile. UNDP refused to
engage in any further discussions with the Centre for Refugee Studies at Moi
University and to date, UNDP has never followed up or addressed the issues raised
in the report. The September 1995 draft report by the Centre for Refugee Studies
was particularly critical of UNDP's interaction with the local NGOs in the WPCC,
the regional coordinating body set up initially by the local NGOs and later taken
over by UNDP. The report concluded:

Given the capacity of UNDP and its national involvement in the
issue of displacement, it was, and still is, probably in the best
position to offer positive support to such a local initiative as
WPCC. However, the general agreement in the field was that
UNDP weakened WPCC considerably, rather than

---

[182]Human Rights Watch/Africa interview with Tecla Wanjala, Coordinator, Peace
and Development Network (Peace-Net), National Council of NGOs, Nairobi, August 8,
1996.

strengthen[ed] it...There was a general lack of understanding on the peoples' part of what UNDP's role was in the Committee...Even after promising to provide for operational costs of WPCC, UNDP was inconsistent in disbursing funds. Of concern to this study was its manner of operation which has been largely unprofessional and uncontractual...Such inconsistencies have greatly weakened the activities of WPCC...As funds and support from UNDP became almost random, the NGO Council on the other hand withdrew its support for WPCC.[183]

The Centre for Refugee Studies report also concluded that:

Perhaps the greatest inconsistency of UNDP came with the Quick Impact Projects ["quips"]. As actors were preparing to launch rehabilitation and reconstruction, UNDP requested them to generate quips for funding...Several quips were generated and approved by WPCC for funding. However, only 3 NGOs: CRWRC [Church Reformed World Relief Committee], International Child Trust (ICT) and Action Nordsud, were funded. This reduced cooperation between other actors and the committee, which was by now perceived as a UNDP body. In spite of these inconsistencies, UNDP did not explain the discrepancies, either to the committee, or individual NGOs. This failure to keep promises, by UNDP, increased resentment towards it and also against WPCC for its ineffectiveness in influencing funding decisions, in their favor, by UNDP. This resentment was translated into distrust of UNDP and falling morale among actors. At the time of the study, UNDP was accused by every respondent of having hijacked the coordination process. In the words of one respondent, "rather than being a member of the committee, UNDP became a commander"...The internal politics within the displaced persons programme at UNDP spilled over, and affected the performance of WPCC. For instance, [UNDP] Field Officers were not properly briefed and this became a constant excuse at WPCC meetings. In the

---

[183]"Western Province Coordination Committee (WPCC): A Performance Appraisal" (draft), presented to UNDP/UNOPS, (Eldoret: Centre for Refugee Studies, Moi University), September 1995, p.47.

end, their whole participation was judged as a failure by all the actors on the ground."[184]

UNDP should have shown greater recognition of the local NGOs' contribution to the internally displaced and should have established a true partnership with them. A component of the UNDP program should have been to increase the capacity of the local groups and to provide them with some measure of protection from the ongoing government harassment that has characterized their work.

No Effort to Seek Long-Term Solutions

"Yes, people wandered back, but not because of anything that UNDP did."
—*International humanitarian worker, Nairobi, August 30, 1996*

Finding lasting solutions to the problem of internal displacement requires attention to the root causes. Those organizations that work with the displaced must have a long-term vision about preventative action and resolution of the issues that led to the violence. The U.N, and UNDP in particular, is well suited to design programs to address the long-term issues that will strengthen development efforts. The question that UNDP needs to ask itself is whether its programs for the displaced are intended only to provide humanitarian relief assistance or whether the agency envisions a more lasting contribution that taps into its development expertise? If it is the latter, then its programs for the internally displaced must address the root causes of the displacement and better engage the host government in implementing the necessary programs.

In Kenya, unresolved land tenure issues dating from the colonial period were a major factor in the government's ability to mobilize members of the Kalenjin and Maasai communities to launch attacks on their neighbors. These tensions were exacerbated by unresolved grievances arising out of post-colonial distribution of land, growing land pressures, and a high population growth that adversely affected traditionally pastoralist groups among others.[185] Issues of land

---

[184]Ibid., p.47-48.

[185]Isaac Lenaola, Hadley H. Jenner, Timothy Wichert, "Land Tenure in Pastoral Lands," African Centre for Technology Studies, *In Land We Trust: Environment, Private Property and Constitutional Change* (Eds. Calestous Juma, J.B. Ojwang), (London and Nairobi: Zed Books and Initiatives Publishers, 1996). pp.231-257.

ownership, acquisition of land, unauthorized plot demarcations and settlement were critical to a sustainable solution to the displaced problem in Kenya. Displaced residents repeatedly informed UNDP that land ownership and scarcity were a major cause of the unrest and needed to be addressed.[186]

UNDP was well aware of the fact that any long-term solution required attention to land tenure issues. Once again, UNDP was unable or unwilling to take any concrete action in the face of government resistance. One of UNDP's stated objectives was "to assist in civil registration in order to maintain an accurate record of the displacees and to initiate systematic land registration."[187] The first Rogge report stated that the Kenyan government had to:

> take forceful steps to ensure that no one loses their rights to own land in any areas settled prior to the clashes. Local administrations must be required to process the speedy issue of land titles in areas where subdivision of farms have been surveyed. Elsewhere, the surveying of subdivisions must be accelerated. Irregularities in the sale of shares by cooperative scheme managements and within local land registry offices need to be more closely and forcefully policed. There should be appropriate administrative measures in place to ensure that land sales be minimized in the clash affected areas for a period of time, pending a just resolution of outstanding clams of ownership and a regularization of displacees access to lands on which they had been living prior to the clashes. A request to donors by the Government for assistance in manpower development and computer application for its land title and surveys offices should be received positively by them.[188]

John Rogge was aware that the land registration system was backlogged, and records were a mess. He also was aware that the irregularities were being exploited by those who had instigated the "ethnic" violence. He did state that the program should find ways to build capacity and accountability in the system, which was

---

[186]UNDP, "UNDP Mission Report," April 18-22, 1995, p.3.

[187]Government of Kenya/UNDP, *Programme Document: Programme for Displaced Persons*, Inter-Agency Joint Programme, October 26, 1993.

[188]Rogge Report I, UNDP, September 1993, part 3(16.2).

currently unable to keep pace with the huge numbers of farms that had been sub divided and needed to be surveyed and registered.[189] The second Rogge report recommended that:

> Where UNDP, in collaboration with the donors, can play an invaluable role regarding the land tenure dilemma, albeit outside the ambit of the DPP [Displaced Persons Program], is in a long-term capacity building of the various government agencies involved in the regulation and allocation of lands. · This involves the Lands Adjudication and Settlement Department, the Surveys Department, and the Land Titles Department. The convoluted system which is in place is hopelessly overburdened, and is unlikely to ever catch up with the existing back-log...UNDP's mandate of capacity building must, therefore, be directed to addressing this urgent problem.[190]

In one of its program proposals, UNDP actually put forward a plan of action which, had it been implemented, would have made a significant contribution to Kenya's long-term development prospects. UNDP had plans that "[t]he difficult issue of land ownership, regularization of land titles and deeds, registration of clash affected victims, will be covered...with provision of training, surveying equipment, transport, legal assistance and organization of registration exercises.   The reallocation of under utilized land will be one of the aspects of the Programme."[191]

Even under normal circumstances, land rights in Kenya are subject to a complicated, overburdened, and outdated set of land tenure and registration laws set out in a complicated web of legal regimes, including English, Indian and customary law. All former "native reserve" areas restricted to Africans during the colonial period are governed under English law with land titles issued under the Registration Land Act. The Government Land Act, drawn from Indian law, governs land in urban areas. Customary law is also operational in some areas. Individual ownership rights are still not traditionally recognized in some areas, for

---

[189]Presentation by John Rogge contained in minutes of the third Excom Meeting, Kenyatta International Conference Centre, Nairobi, September 8, 1994.

[190]Rogge Report II, UNDP, September 1994, part 6.4.

[191]UNDP, "Programme for Displaced Persons and Communities Affected by Ethnic Violence," Nairobi, February 1994, p.7.

example among pastoral and nomadic groups in the Rift Valley and North Eastern Province. Different types of land tenure are governed under settlement schemes, trust land, cooperative/company farms, group ranches and government land.[192] Kenya's land ownership system is hopelessly outdated and backlogged.

The complicated nature of the land laws in Kenya and the weak judicial system have allowed for theft, or "land grabbing" as it is known, to become a national past time among government officials. Land is a scarce and valued commodity that has been used, by the colonial and post-colonial governments in Kenya, as a means to consolidate political power. President Moi's government is no exception in this regard, using corruption and manipulation to acquire and control land for political ends. The "ethnic" violence has furthered this process. The failure to resolve the land crisis in Kenya is a critical impediment to resolving the ethnic tensions inflamed by the recent violence in a long-term manner.

Human Rights Watch recognizes that the issue of land law reform faced resistance from government quarters for obvious reasons. As UNDP points out:

> It is true that the justice and land issue was not resolved. The failure to do so, however, was the responsibility of the government. Both UNDP and other donors (e.g. Germany) offered repeatedly to provide technical assistance for land registration and the reform process. These offers were not

---

[192]Under settlement schemes, administered by the Settlement Fund Trustees, the large tracts of colonial settler land that were sold to the government were surveyed, demarcated into smaller plots, and offered to the landless with a long-term mortgage loan of over twenty years, with an initial down payment of 10 percent. If the scheme is registered, at the end of the mortgage, the person can collect the title and own the land outright. If the scheme is not registered, then outright purchase certificates were given. Trust Land is administered by the Local Councils, but survey and demarcation done by the Ministry of Lands and Settlement. The process is slow and is arbitrated by committees of elders. Appeals are heard by an Arbitration Board and the Minister has the final resort. Titles can only be given where there are no objections. Cooperative farms are owned jointly by a group that pays off the mortgage over time. Group ranch land is administered under the Group Ranch Act which allocated hundreds of thousands of acres as communal land for the pastoralist Maasai community. Adjudication is currently underway to divide and privatize this land so that resident Maasai can sell or lease the land. However, this process has been fraught with corruption as government officials working in the land offices and elsewhere have acquired this land. Government lands are mainly forest area.

accepted. No donor can impose technical assistance when it is
not wanted.[193]

Nevertheless, UNDP has an express mandate to address the issue of land reform,
and in light of the importance of this issue in resolving the Kenyan crisis, it was
incumbent on UNDP to bring pressure to bear on the government. It is not entirely
true that no donor can impose technical assistance when it is not wanted. It is
certainly more difficult, but it is not impossible. There are examples, in the Kenyan
context alone, of the government conceding to pressure from the World Bank or
donors to accept technical assistance, for example, to address government
corruption or to promote structural adjustment policies, such as privatization or
trade liberalization. One former UNDP official who worked on the displaced
persons program concluded that this issue alone holds the key to reintegration:

> The ethnic violence is an issue that will continue to simmer until
> the land registration department is revamped. What we needed
> was a team of competent UNDP consultants to pressure the
> government to take steps in this regard. They were the only ones
> who could have done that. The government is susceptible to
> international pressure. UNDP should have mobilized that
> pressure.[194]

In any program for the internally displaced, UNDP must address the long-
term impediments to reconciliation and reintegration. This issue of land tenure
pressures is a commonly faced impediment to reintegration of internally displaced
populations. As a practical matter, UNDP remains a preeminent, if not the
preeminent entity, to develop strategies to address this issue. Given its development
expertise, it is well-suited to addressing problems such as land tenure pressures,
which are often key to a resolution.

---

[193]See Appendix: UNDP Response, p.5.

[194]Human Rights Watch/Africa interview with David Round-Turner, former Policy
Advisor, UNDP Displaced Persons Program, Nairobi, August 26, 1996.

Damaged Credibility After Abandoning the Displaced

*"Tell UNDP that we are still refugees in Maela. We are still suffering.
Our land has been taken. Our children are not in school. We cannot get
medical care. People are still suffering here. It is a struggle to live."*
—*Kikuyu displaced women, Maela, Nakuru district, August 7, 1996*

Few among those who remain displaced in Kenya have not heard of the UNDP program that was set up to return them to their land. Not surprisingly, the feeling that UNDP abandoned them when the program ended in November 1995 runs deep among those interviewed by Human Rights Watch/Africa. By 1995, the UNDP program was floundering and at a standstill following the government's actions in Maela. Reintegration and reconciliation appeared to be progressing or not, regardless of UNDP's presence. Meanwhile, UNDP had alienated the NGO and donor communities. It had inflated the numbers of estimated returnees all the while asserting that no numbers could be estimated. It was widely perceived to have aligned itself closely with the government regardless of what occurred. It was seen to have countenanced forced dispersals of camps. Its program had never made the transition from short-term relief programs to long-term sustainable development programs. In short, the closure of the UNDP program was not in and of itself a bad thing. It was a recognition that it had been badly compromised because it had never demanded of the government minimum conditions for operation. However, for those who remain displaced, the closure of the UNDP program is still a bitter pill to swallow. The end of an international presence in the rural areas brings with it the realization that what little hope they ever held out for returning to their land is unlikely to materialize.

Human Rights Watch/Africa visited Maela and interviewed some of the displaced who remain there or who had been relocated to Central Province when Maela was cleared by the government in December 1994. Virtually abandoned and still destitute, the remaining displaced reported that no international agency had visited Maela for over a year. The fact that UNDP was so involved in providing services at Maela in 1994 had raised expectations that the large international agency would ensure the safety and eventual reintegration of the displaced there. The displaced were even more crushed that UNDP did little or nothing for them following the dispersal. One displaced man said, "after the government did all that to us, all UNDP did was to come back here in January 1995 and take all their office

equipment and leave."[195]   Ernest Murimi of the Catholic Justice and Peace
Commission said: "UNDP cannot come back in here.   The program failed
miserably and there is no trust in them."[196]

For all the flurry around Maela, little was actually done by UNDP to
negotiate the return of those forcibly removed from Maela and to provide redress.
As far as Human Rights Watch/Africa was able to determine, no security officers
were ever disciplined for their mistreatment of the displaced at Maela. Some of
those displaced who were dumped in Central Province made their own way back
to Maela. One of those displaced recounted what had happened to him:

> I was on a lorry with 145 other people. We were made to leave
> our belongings behind. We were taken to Central Province and
> left near the D.O's office. We weren't given anything. I asked
> an administration policeman where we were supposed to go. He
> pointed to a forest nearby. We stayed there for two weeks. MSF
> [Medecins sans Frontieres (Spain)] helped us. The D.O's office
> then told us that it was illegal for us to be there. We were taken
> to Ol Kalou, then to Tumaini. We were not given any assistance
> the whole time. I used to have a two-acre plot in Enosupukia.
> Now, I will never have anything. My message to UNDP is:
> Don't forget us. Fulfill your promises to us. Among the clash
> victims, only a few have been resettled. Even the land that was
> given to some of the displaced [200 families at Ol Kalou] has
> been taken by the government. The chief got twenty acres, the
> P.C. got 100 acres and the D.C. got some.[197]

International responsibility for the internally displaced, once embarked on,
should not be administered in this manner. For many of the displaced, the
international presence is the only hope they have that something will be done to

---

[195]Human Rights Watch/Africa interview with displaced (Kikuyu) man, Maela,
Nakuru District, Rift Valley Province, August 7, 1996.

[196]Human Rights Watch/Africa interview, Ernest Murimi with Executive
Secretary, Justice and Peace Commission, Catholic Diocese of Nakuru, Nakuru, August 6,
1996.

[197]Human Rights Watch/Africa interview with displaced (Kikuyu) man, Maela,
Nakuru District, Rift Valley Province, August 7, 1996.

ameliorate their dire situation. UNDP should ensure that in the future, contingency planning provides for alternatives, including political and financial support for NGOs, should it need to pull out or should it be expelled.

After UNDP: The Current Situation Facing Kenya's Internally Displaced

The Kenyan government has used violence to remain in power by punishing and disenfranchising opposition supporters, while rewarding its supporters from the Kalenjin and Maasai groups with illegally obtained land. It has also successfully driven thousands of Kikuyus, Luos, and Luhyas from land that is politically and economically valuable. The government, although distancing itself publicly from calls for the introduction of majimboism (ethnic federalism), has promoted a majimbo policy by strengthening the Rift Valley Province as an ethnically-defined regional base for those in power: new institutions and services include Moi University, a military college, a branch of the Central Bank of Kenya, an ammunitions factory and an international airport in Eldoret. Moreover, the threat of renewed violence continues to haunt those who have returned to their land—a strong message to potential opposition supporters in the next election due to be held by early 1998. The after-effects of the ethnic clashes continue to be seen in the ethnically fractured and volatile political climate that the government still manipulates to its ends. Relying on other forms of repression as well as the disarray and divisions within the political opposition, the Moi government has had less need to rely on the tactics of terror and bloodshed to ensure its incumbency.

The lack of data on the displaced has had tragic consequences for those who remain off their land. Many of those who are still displaced come from areas such as Olenguruone, Enosupukia, and Mt. Elgon where the remaining Kalenjin and Maasai residents have sworn not to allow other ethnic groups to return to their land, and the government has shown no signs of taking any action to put an end to this ethnic expulsion. Most of these displaced have drifted to other areas of the country to become agricultural day laborers or to urban areas in search of work. Others have become part of the unemployed poor, adding to the alarming levels of crime in Kenya largely caused by poverty and government mismanagement of resources. In 1995, UNDP had estimated that there were about 50,000 people living in "very temporary refuges" or "surviving in peri-urban slum areas," who have been "overlooked" because of the difficulty of finding satisfactory and quick solutions.[198] It is likely that this number is even higher now. It is unrealistic to believe that specific programs can be introduced for the urban displaced living in

---

[198]UNDP Office for Project Services, "1995 Inception Report, Internally Displaced Persons Programme," Nairobi, 1995.

the slums of Nairobi or even in Nakuru or Kisumu. In these larger urban areas, the best that can realistically be undertaken is to ensure that such displacees are included within existing programs for urban slum populations. However, UNDP should ensure that any such programs do not further the government's policy of reintegration of the displaced outside of the Rift Valley Province.

Abandoned and forgotten by the international community, and victims of their own government, Kenya's internally displaced seem destined to become a permanently disenfranchised underclass.

9. LOOKING TO THE FUTURE

Addressing the Gaps in UNDP

It is demanding a lot of any existing U.N. agency to provide programs that meet all the needs of displaced populations. However, it is not unreasonable to expect that the U.N. agencies tasked with the care of internally displaced populations would seek to draw on their strengths in providing services to the displaced, while acknowledging and addressing their weaknesses. In this way, through shared expertise and learned lessons, a standardized institutional expertise within the various agencies dealing with the internally displaced would be developed over time. This process requires an active effort by the institution to draw on outside expertise where appropriate, while building an in-house capacity. With each completed program, the agency can take a hard look at the results and assess its successes and failures in order to strengthen future activities.

UNDP does have a role to play in administering programs for the internally displaced. It brings unique and valuable contribution to this area. UNDP is an agency with extensive experience in issues pertaining to community reintegration, poverty alleviation, land tenure, and sustainable development. UNDP's development mandate also allows it to bring a broader, longer-term vision to emergency programs which, if lacking, can create or reinforce food relief dependencies among uprooted populations. Further, UNDP's permanent presence in a country and its familiarity with a country can also strengthen its ability to successfully implement programs.

Conversely, UNDP has relatively little experience in emergency work, conflict resolution processes, human rights and humanitarian principles, or protection assistance—all prerequisites to a successful reintegration program for populations whose displacement is linked to government abuse or civil unrest. The gaps in UNDP's institutional capacity do not inherently preclude it from successfully assisting internally displaced populations. In fact, these gaps are illustrative of the existing deficiencies in the international system more generally regarding a holistic approach to displaced populations—there is no existing agency that can fully address all the needs (immediate and long-term) of the displaced. The point, however, is not that UNDP is lacking certain areas of expertise with regard to the internally displaced, but that as an institution it appeared unwilling or unable to expand and evolve its capacity fully to address the situation in Kenya. UNDP not only overlooked its own past experiences in implementing programs for the internally displaced, but also did not actively seek to address or supplement the institutional weaknesses that became apparent as the program unfolded. It is also unclear whether the lessons learned from the Kenyan program have prompted

UNDP to make any institutional changes toward improving its implementation of internally displaced programs for the future.

There are identifiable factors that contributed to the problems encountered in UNDP's Displaced Persons Program in Kenya, which, if addressed by UNDP, could significantly strengthen its future implementation of such programs. The Kenyan experience indicates that specific elements need to be in place for such a mission to succeed: a contract with the government, which sets out minimum conditions for engagement; a plan for data collection and dissemination; human rights monitoring and advocacy; a protection component; and a method for drawing on inter-agency expertise.

First and foremost, the leadership at UNDP must take the necessary steps to respond to the expanded responsibilities that come with its designation as an agency that administers programs for the internally displaced. This process requires a committed examination of UNDP's traditional operating practices to determine where it needs to adopt a different working approach as well as to develop capacity in the areas where it lacks experience. UNDP has already begun this process, acknowledging and identifying in its policy documents that human rights, social justice and land reform are critical factors in reintegration efforts. The UNDP management must now take the next step and adopt an approach that integrates assistance, prevention, protection, human rights, and development components into the implementation of its programs for the displaced. In doing so, UNDP will need to provide training to existing staff and may also require the addition of specialized staff to supplement field staff in certain skills. If UNDP does not possess or decides not to develop an in-house expertise, it should be willing to genuinely coordinate and cooperate with other U.N. agencies to ensure that its programs are comprehensive.

UNDP needs to prioritize data collection and dissemination as part of its programs. In order to do this, UNDP needs to develop better tools to monitor and evaluate the condition of the displaced. Without underestimating the difficulty of collecting such information, UNDP should as best as possible ensure that it creates a systematic monitoring system to collect aggregate numbers (and names where possible) and to document the condition of the displaced. The information should include conditions of physical need as well as protection issues. UNDP should create a mechanism to disseminate this information on a regular basis within the U.N. system as well as to other relevant local and international agencies.

UNDP needs to strengthen its capacity to promote and protect human rights. UNDP's projects, while having human rights implications, have not traditionally required the agency to develop expertise in human rights reporting and advocacy work, nor to view human rights promotion and protection as a central part of its mandate. Frequently, displacement is caused by human rights violations and, as often, reintegration and rehabilitation solutions are integrally linked to the resolution of human rights and protection issues. In these programs probably more than any others, human rights considerations cannot be dispensed with in order to further good relations with a government or to secure other operational goals. UNDP should be responsible for vigorous advocacy efforts at the local, national and international levels to protect the rights of the displaced. If quiet representations to the government or controlling authority are unsuccessful, UNDP should adopt more public protests.

The absence of a strong human rights component in UNDP's work has been attributed primarily to the fact that this area has not traditionally been seen to be a priority of UNDP's development work. There is a widespread perception within UNDP that human rights work is not development work, despite the fact that the building of development processes to promote democratization of government and to strengthen institutions and processes for disclosure of information, access, and due process are all development goals with human rights implications. Another reason offered for UNDP's downplaying of human rights is the premium placed on the appearance of neutrality. Rather than be outspoken on issues that would be sure to earn a government's ire, UNDP appears to conceive of its role as that of a neutral implementor of a reintegration program devoid of any potential political tensions. Some in UNDP justify silence on human rights issues by arguing that channels of communication with a government should be kept open in order to further the cause of the displaced. The misperception that human rights issues should be left to the human rights agencies in the U.N. must be actively overcome by UNDP, particularly where human rights concerns can impede a lasting solution for a displaced population.[199] This policy change must be given the necessary political support at the highest levels of UNDP to alter these widely held misperceptions about human rights work within the agency.

UNDP needs to develop and incorporate protection responsibilities in the implementation of its programs for the internally displaced. Unlike many other development projects in which UNDP is involved worldwide, programs that deal with the internally displaced are made more difficult by the security and political issues surrounding the nature of their displacement. Protection issues with the displaced come up both with regard to ensuring physical security from threats of

---

[199]The recent statement by Secretary-General Kofi Annan that he considers human rights to be an integral part of all main areas of U.N. activities, including its development work, is a step in the right direction. "UN Reform: The First Six Weeks," Statement by Kofi Annan, U.N. Secretary-General, New York, February 13, 1997.

coercion and violence, and the longer term issues of defending legal rights that were violated by those responsible for the displacement. While the responsibility for providing protection ultimately rests with governments, UNDP has a role to play in making this a priority with governments, training government officials on human rights and humanitarian standards, and advocating vigorously for safety for the displaced. UNDP has traditionally not taken on a protection role that requires it to be critical of a government's abuses against its people. However, as UNDP continues to administer programs for the internally displaced, it will have to deal with the inevitable tensions that arise between seeking to provide protection to the displaced while attempting to work with the very government that often caused the displacement. The narrow operating space requires a skilled and careful balancing act between being critical of government policies while relying on government assistance to provide the political will and security for reintegration. Few, if any, UNDP staff have expertise on how to deal with the physical safety of the displaced, even in places where protection issues are paramount. In this regard, there are some lessons that UNDP can learn from UNHCR, which has extensive experience in this area.[200]

UNDP needs to be prepared to transform its political relationships with governments, when necessary, to protest government policies against the displaced. UNDP has traditionally worked very closely with governments in order to undertake its programs. Having to work governments on its other development projects, UNDP resident representatives may be reluctant to compromise their position and programs in the country by speaking out on human rights and protection issues. Thorny human rights and protection issues appear to be seen as too sensitive a matter to push with errant governments. In Kenya, the attitude adopted was that if UNDP wanted to remain operational, it had to approach any

---

[200]UNDP is already taking steps to finalize a new framework for operational coordination with UNHCR for returning refugees. Something similar should be initiated for reintegration programs for the internally displaced. The objectives of the agreement with UNHCR for refugees are to "promote early warning; address the negative effect of large inflows of refugees; promote community-level recovery, peace-building and reconciliation; reinforce the linkages between initial reintegration needs of returning refugees and those of other groups in their areas of return, with a view to ensuring sustainable development in such areas; to foster an early and smooth phase-out of humanitarian assistance in favour of sustainable local development; and to work jointly to mobilize national [and] international resources for measures designed to attain the above objectives." " Further Elaboration on Follow-up to Economic and Social Council Resolution 1995/56: Strengthening of the Coordination of Emergency Humanitarian Assistance," U.N. Doc. DP/1997/CRP.10, February 28, 1997, para. 22.

government abuses diplomatically and distance itself from those groups (mainly NGOs) publicly criticizing the government's abuses toward the displaced. This translated into little or no pressure on the government from the one actor which arguably had the most influence with the government to address the human rights issues integral to lasting solutions. Having not handled human rights issues on a regular basis, UNDP has also not dealt extensively with the attendant angry responses that such work usually generates from the offending government. At the moment, the institutional instinct to avoid controversy with a government results in sidestepping crucial human rights and protection issues instead of making them a fundamental starting point for resolving situations of internal displacement.

UNDP should take steps to address the inherent tension that inevitably arises when a UNDP resident representative, with a close working relationship with a government, is designated as a resident coordinator of an emergency program dealing with the displaced. As a resident coordinator, that person may be required to take on a more critical role of government policy in order to advocate on behalf of the displaced. A U.N. official working on internally displaced issues at DHA identified a major problem related to UNDP's involvement in programs for the internally displaced:

> The way the programs are currently structured brings an inherent tension into the role that the UNDP resident representative is being asked to play. On the one hand, that person is being asked to work closely with the government on all development projects and to foster a good relationship. Then you are asking that same person to put on another hat when they are the resident coordinator of an emergency program and criticize the government for human rights violations against the internally displaced. The government is obviously not happy about that and complains. Promotions in UNDP are predicated on good relations with the government. A resident representative who is doing a good job for the internally displaced is probably not doing good things for their career.[201]

Further complicating the situation is the fact that DHA plays a role once a resident representative is designated a resident coordinator. A resident representative/ resident coordinator may be put in the difficult professional position of receiving

---

[201]Human Rights Watch/Africa interview with DHA official (name withheld on request), New York, February 26, 1997.

differing instructions on how best to proceed from UNDP and DHA. UNDP needs to give the necessary support and direction to its resident representatives/resident coordinators to ensure that this institutional dilemma does not undermine programmatic goals with regard to the displaced.

UNDP needs to provide training and direction to its staff, particularly resident representatives, in the areas where there is relatively less in-house expertise, such as human rights and protection responsibilities. The mistakes of the Kenya operation went unchallenged by the policymakers at UNDP headquarters for the duration of the program. There appeared to be little institutional attention to the unfolding problems or any attention given to the fact that the program needed direction. UNDP is planning to decentralize its programs to the field offices.[202] However, in doing so, it must ensure that its field staff are properly trained and equipped to take on the task of implementing such programs.

Lastly, successes and failures of past programs should be examined and utilized to strengthen future programs. The findings of this examination process must be actively incorporated into programs for the internally displaced through a systematic institutional procedure. For instance, the complete absence of a human rights component in the UNDP program in Kenya is all the more puzzling given that a prior UNDP program for the reintegration of displaced populations in Central America was widely viewed as a success, in large part because it prioritized the promotion and protection of human rights as a central component of that program. The Development Program for Displaced Persons, Refugees, and Returnees in Central America (PRODERE), executed by UNDP between 1989 and 1995, was created to promote and facilitate the social and economic reintegration of more than two million people uprooted by regional conflicts in the 1980s. Initially a three-year program, PRODERE was extended two years until the end of July 1995. PRODERE was the largest single program ever executed by UNDP/OPS.

PRODERE's program consisted of an approach that addressed the root causes of the conflict and created a basis for sustainable development. PRODERE also promoted the creation of local institutions that remained in place after the closure of the program to provide services in areas such as production, employment, income-generation, promotion of human rights, health, and

---

[202]"Further Elaboration on Follow-up to Economic and Social Council Resolution 1995/56: Strengthening of the Coordination of Emergency Humanitarian Assistance," U.N. Doc. DP/1997/CRP.10, February 28, 1997, para. 11.

education.[203]   The perceived success of the PRODERE program is in large part due to its approach, which recognized that the program "must grant the highest priority to the promotion of human rights, as an indispensable component of the development, peace and democracy process in Central America."[204] Notwithstanding its own problems, PRODERE was credited not only with strengthening national human rights institutions, but promoting the creation of grassroots human rights activities that helped change the local human rights culture. Among other human rights activities, PRODERE provided training and technical assistance for human rights monitors, creating a network of local people who could assist victims to bring cases through the judicial system; it disseminated human rights information in Spanish and indigenous languages; and brought together local human rights groups with government and law enforcement officials. Yet, where were the lessons of PRODERE reflected in the UNDP Kenya program? While it is clear that it was not a simple matter of replicating PRODERE in Kenya, there were important lessons that PRODERE offered UNDP. UNDP did send over some Kenyan government officials and UNDP staff to Central America at the outset of the program.[205] However, little of the expertise and positive experiences that UNDP had developed in Central America appeared to have been translated to the Kenyan context.

---

[203]PRODERE operated as six national sub-programs and three regional sub-programs. The six country sub-programs—Guatemala, Belize, El Salvador, Honduras, Nicaragua and Costa Rica—had either two or three areas of intervention per country. The size and budget of the national sub-programs varied, depending upon national characteristics. Greatest priority was assigned to refugee-producing countries preparing for long-term reintegration programs. Guatemala, El Salvador, and Nicaragua were each allocated $23 million over the duration of the program. Costa Rica was allocated $7 million, Honduras $5 million, and Belize $3 million. At its height in 1992, PRODERE's annual budget reached over $35 million, with over 500 employees, including international staff, local experts, U.N. volunteers, administrative support staff, and drivers. Peter Sollis and Christina M. Schultz, "Lessons of the PRODERE Experience in Central America," (Washington D.C.: Refugee Policy Group, November 1995).

[204]Joint Declaration of PRODERE by the Italian government Delegation and UNDP, Guatemala City, November 19, 1991, as quoted in Ibid., p.7.

[205]Human Rights Watch/Africa interview with UNDP official (name withheld on request), New York, February 26, 1997.

Lack of a Strong Integrated U.N. Framework to Protect the Displaced

The U.N. is well-positioned to take the lead in designing international mechanisms to improve protection and assistance to the internally displaced. As the Kenyan example indicates, the U.N. can facilitate negotiations and support from the government and local authorities. It can bring together diverse groups and coordinate efforts. U.N. interlocutors can be an important link in terms of communication, information sharing, and consultation. However, U.N. programs for the displaced should not be embarked on without an understanding of what needs should be addressed and the strengths and weaknesses of the organizations tasked to deal with the situation.

The ability of the international community to offer effective assistance and protection to internally displaced populations will remain inadequate as long as there is a lack of a clearly designated institutional mandate within the U.N. to assist the internally displaced. Although shared responsibility by the various U.N. agencies that have undertaken programs on behalf of the displaced is not the problem *per se*, the manner in which this arrangement has evolved has resulted in a series of separate agency programs—none of which seem to be benefitting from the expertise of the other. The needs of the internally displaced span the spectrum from emergency humanitarian relief to economic development and reintegration. Since no one agency is solely tasked with the internally displaced, all the agencies currently dealing with displaced programs are lacking some capacity to administer certain aspects along this broad spectrum. In particular, the issue of protection appears to be most neglected. What is required is a more systematic approach which consolidates and builds on the U.N.'s capacity so that identifiable elements (such as protection, documentation, human rights reporting and legal assistance) that are critical for programs for the internally displaced are automatically incorporated into all programs.

The lack of a clear mandate for assistance, protection and long-term solutions with regard to the internally displaced is a problem that will continue to plague those U.N. agencies attempting to deal with them. In the absence of a clear mandate, U.N. agencies are not sure how to relate in given circumstances as lines of responsibility and accountability are not clear. The *ad hoc* mandates of the U.N. agencies given the responsibility of dealing with the internally displaced are an inappropriate substitute for the creation of a regularized system.

For instance, UNHCR's core mandate for refugees has resulted in a regular and defined mechanism to address the protection problems facing that group of uprooted people. UNHCR has comparatively much more experience than UNDP in working with governments to provide protection to refugee populations. It has developed standards, criteria, and training programs which have enhanced its ability to offer protection to refugee populations over the years. Similarly, it has a wealth of experience in dealing with hostile and recalcitrant host governments on which it must rely to ensure refugee protection.[206] Yet although internally displaced populations are facing comparable conditions, no system is in place to ensure that similar protection steps are being taken by other agencies working on the displaced. For instance, in Kenya, protection issues should have been a priority since the government itself had been responsible for instigating and condoning the violence, and because security forces had not provided protection. Yet, UNDP does not have extensive experience with protection. This should have been anticipated.

In the Kenyan example, the UNDP program appeared to function as a completely internal UNDP project, rather than as part of a broader U.N. program for the internally displaced. It appeared to have little or no genuine collaboration with other U.N. agencies, including DHA, and sought or benefitted little from obtaining direction or expertise available from other agencies within the U.N. Other U.N. agencies, such as UNICEF, that wanted to become more involved in the Displaced Persons Program in Kenya were neither encouraged to nor able to contribute in the manner in which they wanted to.[207] Other U.N. agencies that should have been consulted were not. For example, within Kenya alone there were two U.N. agencies dealing with the forcibly displaced between 1993 and 1995: UNHCR dealing with Somali, Sudanese and Ethiopian refugees predominantly in the North-Eastern Province, and UNDP dealing with the Kenyan internally displaced in Rift Valley, Western and Nyanza Provinces. In both situations,

---

[206]That is not to say that UNHCR is an ideal role model in this regard, but rather to note that compared to UNDP, UNHCR has more experience in this area. Protection of refugee and asylum-seekers around the world has deteriorated over the past couple of decades. Against the backdrop of a global retrenchment against refugees by host governments, UNHCR has sought to shift the focus of solutions for refugee crises from the exile-oriented strategies of the past to an emphasis on voluntary repatriation as the durable solution of choice, and on the prevention of refugee flows and the containment of refugee crises. This shift toward return-oriented solutions frequently conflicts with UNHCR's basic protection role in the context of voluntary repatriation, and has resulted in an erosion of the protection standards set forth in certain conclusions of its Executive Committee and in other public statements. See Human Rights Watch, "Uncertain Refuge: International Failures to Protect Refugees," *A Human Rights Watch Short Report*, vol. 9, no. 1(G), April 1997.

[207]Human Rights Watch/Africa telephone interview with a diplomat (name and location withheld by request), March 12, 1997.

security and protection for the victims was a problem.[208] In both situations, the government was hostile to the populations. In one situation, publicity and active pressure was placed on the government by UNHCR, which resulted in positive changes in the situation of refugees in Kenya.[209] In the other, private engagement and public silence on the situation of the displaced by UNDP resulted in no change in government policy. While the two situations are not identical, this example

---

[208]In 1993, Human Rights Watch visited the camps and documented testimonies of rape survivors and the inadequate response of the Kenyan government and UNHCR to provide protection and security for the refugee population located in an insecure area close to the Somali border. Many of those interviewed had been gang-raped at gunpoint, some by as many as seven men. In the vast majority of cases, rape victims were also robbed, severely beaten, knifed, or shot. Most refugee women were at risk of rape from Somali-Kenyan bandits joined by former Somali soldiers or fighters from Somalia who crossed the Kenya-Somali border to launch raids. A small portion of the rapes were committed by Kenyan police officers and other refugees. Human Rights Watch also documented the lack of adequate investigation and prosecution of rape which contributed to the situation of lawlessness and impunity. Human Rights Watch/Women's Rights Project and Africa division, "Seeking Refuge, Finding Terror: The Widespread Rape of Somali Women Refugees in North Eastern Kenya," *A Human Rights Watch/Africa Short Report*, vol. 5, no. 13, October 1993.

[209]Follow-up visits by Human Rights Watch/Africa Women's Rights Project to the refugee camps in Kenya in 1994 and 1996 found important changes as a result of UNHCR's advocacy work towards the Kenyan government. Among other things, UNHCR organized fencing around the camps to discourage incursions by bandits and took measures to confer greater responsibility on the refugees for establishing security in their camps. UNHCR conducted human rights training for Kenyan police officers and took other steps to offer material support for Kenyan law enforcement, including the construction of a police post near the refugee camps. In turn, the Kenyan government augmented the police presence in the area from fifty to 250 and began conducting bi-monthly helicopter patrols. Counseling and medical and legal services were instituted for rape survivors, and procedures were put into place by UNHCR to ensure that medical and police reports are filed as a matter of routine practice. As a result, the number of reported rapes of refugee women and children virtually halved from 200 cases in 1993 to seventy-six in 1994 and seventy in 1995. Several prosecutions of rapists resulted in convictions by 1996. In addition, refugees interviewed by Human Rights Watch spoke of improved confidence in the security of their camps. While rape has by no means been eradicated in the refugee camps in northeastern Kenya, the improvements in the situation indicate that decisive action on the part of UNHCR and thoughtful protection programs can bring change. See Human Rights Watch, "Uncertain Refuge: International Failures to Protect Refugees," *A Human Rights Watch Short Report*, vol. 9, no. 1(G), April 1997, pp.15-18.

indicates that this government responded only when publicly and actively pushed to do so. Yet, UNDP did not collaborate or cooperate with UNHCR to discuss ways in which protection for the internally displaced might be improved.

In the area of protection, UNHCR has by far the best developed standards, rules of conduct, and practical guidelines for planning and implementation of its refugee programs. Many of these are transferable to situations of internal displacement. There is much more scope for U.N. agencies to look to UNHCR for guidance in this area. UNHCR has distinctly relevant experience in dealing with the issues facing uprooted people. Other U.N. agencies can benefit from this expertise through cooperation and coordination with UNHCR. However, increasing UNHCR involvement cannot be done as a cynical means through which to contain refugee populations within their country of origin to avoid having to provide international protection, including asylum. Some states have advocated increased UNHCR involvement with the internally displaced as a means to preempt such populations from becoming refugee populations with the incumbent responsibilities on states to provide asylum. There is considerable apprehension among refugee protection circles that increased protection for internally displaced persons may be used as a way to contain refugee flows in order to diminish international responsibility for providing protection and asylum to refugee populations. This valid concern should not, however, result in less protection for the internally displaced, but rather a search for balanced solutions to the problems of both refugee and internally displaced populations, which do not undermine the refugee protection framework.

There is no reason why UNDP, or any other U.N. agencies, should be in the position of having to blunder through areas where they have traditionally not developed an institutional capacity, particularly when that developed expertise already exists in other agencies within the U.N. Enhanced inter-agency collaboration is an important factor in improving services to the internally displaced. Although the UNDP PRODERE reintegration program in Central America benefitted from inter-agency collaboration,[210] as a rule most U.N. inter-agency work is fraught with misgivings, personality clashes, and turf battles. Inter-agency collaboration within the U.N. remains weak and fractured. If the U.N. is to continue its practice of designating a variety of different U.N. agencies to take

---

[210]PRODERE was the first time that four agencies—UNDP, UNHCR, WHO and the International Labor Organization (ILO)—participated in the same program. This arrangement was insisted upon by the donor, the Italian government. The choice of UNDP as the lead agency was determined by its close links to governments and the accumulated experience of OPS, its operating arm.

responsibility for internally displaced populations, the organization must actively improve inter-agency collaboration. This will require sustained attention to create incentives and conditions within the organization for genuine inter-agency collaboration to solve or address the problems of the internally displaced.

Effective coordination and cooperation is the major challenge to developing an institutional capacity that transcends all the U.N.'s agencies and addresses the integral issues connected to the internally displaced. The existence of DHA and the Inter-Agency Task Force on the Internally Displaced do not appear to translate into a genuine leadership or overseeing role once a program is under way. In the Kenyan case, UNDP program administrators and field officers were given no training to develop expertise in human rights or protection issues. Furthermore, little or no cross-agency assistance appeared to have been offered or sought from within the broader U.N. which might have been able to strengthen the UNDP program or to put pressure on the Kenyan government to comply. Unfortunately, this problem is as valid today as it was a few years ago before UNDP embarked on its displaced program in Kenya. Until the U.N. begins to systematize and institutionalize its programs for the displaced, the same blunders and omissions will continue to surface, at the expense of those who can least afford it—the internally displaced.

APPENDIX
UNDP'S RESPONSE TO HUMAN RIGHTS WATCH/AFRICA

The Administrator   United Nations Development Programme

Dear Mr. Takirambudde,

We have now reviewed those sections that you have sent us of the draft report prepared by Human Rights Watch entitled: "Failing the Internally Displaced: the UNDP Displaced Persons Programme In Kenya". I would very much welcome an opportunity to meet with you personally to discuss the report as I believe that both UNDP and Human Rights Watch have much to gain from a balanced assessment of the Kenya IDP programme. My office will contact you to arrange a mutually convenient time for us to meet.

In the meantime, in order to meet your deadline for comments on the report, I am sending you under cover of this letter a note which summarizes UNDP's response to a number of the erroneous assertions and claims made in the draft report. I very much hope that these comments will be fully taken into account in the final published document as we consider that the report, as it is now drafted, contains serious flaws. Let me add that there are a number of individuals knowledgeable about the Kenya programme who appear not to have been consulted by HRW in the preparation of the Report; we would be pleased to give you the names of several people whom HRW might wish to contact in order to round out your assessment.

UNDP does not claim that the Kenya IDP programme was without any shortcomings. We recognise that certain aspects of the programme could have been handled better. We will learn from that experience for the benefit of any future IDP programmes that we may be called upon to assist.

However, in making its judgments about the Kenya IDP programme and UNDP's role in funding and coordinating it, we ask HRW to keep in mind that the programme did help many thousands of Kenyans to return to their land and homes. They could not have done so without the support of this programme and the initiative of the UN Resident Coordinator, David Whaley.

Our attached comments attempt to set the record straight on the most serious, if not all, of the assertions which we believe to be wrong. But more importantly, we request

../..

Mr. Peter Takirambudde
Executive Director
Human Rights Watch
485 Fifth Avenue
New York, N.Y. 10017-6104

-2 -

HRW to take account of the complex political and social environment in which the Kenya IDP programme was developed and implemented as well as the results that it obtained:

-     the UN was faced with a huge humanitarian problem in the Rift Valley which was causing widespread suffering and misery;

-     UNDP, acting through the local UN inter-agency disaster management team, took the lead in trying to do something about this situation. Had UNDP not done so, many, probably most, would still be living in makeshift camps. As is, many thousands of the IDP's have been able to return home;

-     programmes to return the IDP's could not have been launched or conducted effectively without the active involvement and cooperation of the Kenyan government;

-     the atmosphere in Kenya at the time was highly charged, exacerbating ethnic tensions; the country was caught up in a complex problem with complex causes (including land-hunger, over-population and disputes over land use);

-     UNDP, other agencies and NGOs were therefore working in a politically difficult and emotionally-charged environment. All did their best to navigate through the many obstacles in order to return the IDP's to their land and homes. Unfortunately, threading one's way between obstacles rarely means taking a straight line;

As I said above, I very much want UNDP to learn from this experience. For that reason, I propose that we organise a UNDP/HRW workshop to examine the lessons that have been distilled from the Kenya programme. In my view this would be a more constructive approach than a prolonged and acrimonious exchange of correspondence on the specific contents of the report.

I look forward to meeting with you to continue our dialogue.

Yours sincerely,

James Gustave Speth

UNDP RESPONSE

TO

HUMAN RIGHTS WATCH REPORT

FAILING THE INTERNALLY DISPLACED:
THE UNDP PROGRAMME
IN KENYA

UNITED NATIONS DEVELOPMENT PROGRAMME
April 1997

The comments that follow on the draft HRW report do not attempt to refute or rebut all the statements made in the report with which UNDP disagrees. Rather it focuses on several key points where UNDP believes serious errors of fact or interpretation have been made by the authors of the report.

1. Origins of the GOK-UN Program:

In March-April of 1993, the United Nations Disaster Management Team [UNDMT] in Kenya received reports of continued suffering among populations displaced through ethnic clashes in the Rift Valley despite the denial by the Government of any significant problem. The UN team decided to consider whether the experience previously acquired through the drought alleviation programme could be applied to the search for solutions to the ethnic violence in the Rift Valley. The UNDMT hoped to build on the good-will, methodology, and team work with local administrations, NGO's, community groups and donors developed in the drought programme.

The UN team announced to the Government that they would undertake a joint visit to the areas affected by the clashes. This was accepted by the Government which placed no obstacles whatsoever in the way of the team visiting and discussing with a wide range of partners - affected communities, the churches and NGO's working with them, the local administration.

The team was able in May 1993 to visit extensively and to record the situation referred to on page 30 of the HRW report[1]. The report concluded that conditions were far worse and the numbers of persons displaced far greater than the Government realised and recommended urgent action to address their needs.

The mission also enabled the UN team members to assess the needs of the population. Those needs were found to be not so much for short-term humanitarian relief[2], but rather those aspects of the situation which NGO's and churches felt they could not handle alone. The main problems revolved around - security, registration, land-tenure problems, and long-term development goals.

The UN team agreed that these problems could not be solved by the population alone, supported by NGO's and church communities but required the participation of the local and national administration. Without a commitment by the Government to ensure safety, to clearly condemn ethnic violence, to tackle

---

[1] The footnote gives an inaccurate description of this composition - Ferguson and Palmer were both UNVs assigned to the Emergency Relief Unit, funded through DHA and operating under the responsibility of the UNDMT- they were not part of the UNDP team but reported to all the agencies who participated in the mission as well as those who were unable to do so but who reviewed and endorsed the conclusion of the mission

[2] This was already being provided under EU sponsored NGO and church feeding programmes and through local acts of solidarity

the underlying causes of the conflict and to foster long-term development there could be no prospect of return for the majority of the displaced persons nor lasting solution to the crises that had occurred in 1992. These conclusions were shared by the persons consulted on the ground including the Roman Catholic Bishop of Nakuru and Eldoret, who urged the UN team to involve the Government in the search for solutions, stressing that the UN was better placed to raise this issue than others.

John Rogge, a UNDP Consultant at the time, visited the clash areas and produced a report in September 1993. On the basis of this report a GOK-UN programme was developed and approved by Government towards the end of the year.

The UN programme was based on the principle of the community finding its own way back to harmony and coexistence and the value of locally initiated rehabilitation and development activities. It fully recognised the important role of churches and NGO's in the provision of relief, based on their acceptance by the communities and their critical input to the process of reconciliation.

On the other hand, the UN programme also recognised the need for the Government to address issues of security, access, registration and longer term problems - particularly of land-tenure. It recognised as well the need for sustained - though preferably discreet - donor support and informal monitoring through the United Nations.

2. The Rogge Reports :

The HRW report makes numerous factual errors and distortions with regards to the two reports by John Rogge:

HRW page 33: It is incorrect that that Rogge returned for two weeks. He had a five (5) week contract and spent well over three weeks revisiting all the clash affected areas; also on page 33, it is true, as suggested, that the 'report was upbeat' since violence had been reduced greatly over what existed a year earlier and many people were in varying stages of return, i.e., there was a cause to be optimistic.

It also states correctly that Rogge indicated several areas where conditions were still very tenuous [p. 34]. The UN programme's response was based upon these prevailing conditions; the fact that violence surged in a few areas because of a small group of powerful, manipulative politicians cannot be put at the doorstep of UNDP or the UN system. It is ingenuous to suggest that the UN programme's optimistic attitude in early 1994 was inappropriate because the government reverted to its former policy which contributed to an escalation of violence in late 1995;

HRW page 36: It is incorrect to refer to Rogge's assessment as 'rosy'. The report indicates clearly that there were certain high level government officials who were supportive of UNDP's initiative while others were undermining it. Rather the Rogge assessment merely reflected the fact that in two of the three most affected Provinces (Nyanza and Western) there was a gradual return to normalcy.

HRW page 43: refers to the UNDP Programme not 'deterring messages of ethnic hatred', however odious, from being disseminated. How could it? The Rogge report in 1994 clearly indicates that there were numerous politicians who were still actively inciting political violence. What the HRW seems to be unaware of is that the UN Resident Co-ordinator, David Whaley, was consistently bringing these incidents to the attention of Government.

HRW page 5I: what the report leaves out is that the UN programme initiated regular local and regional community meetings where many of these issues were raised. The Rogge report makes reference to the conciliatory role these meetings played and where Government officials, politicians, NGO's and local community representatives regularly interacted. No mention is made in the HRW report of the contribution made by the UN programme in introducing these mediation fora.

HRW page 6I: the report suggests that what was required was a UNDP programme which 'blended immediate assistance with longer term rehabilitation and development strategies'. This is a misrepresentation of the purpose of the UN programme. It was a rehabilitation programme.

Indeed the Rogge report devotes a whole chapter on the rehabilitation aspect of the programme. Moreover, Rogge reported that during his field visits, he disagreed with some of the church groups and NGOs who insisted on continuing with relief programmes, while the UN programme was trying to promote rehabilitation and recovery.

HRW page 62: The point made about the second Rogge report 'whitewashing' the problems with the UN programme is untrue. The central thesis in the second report was that the church and church-based NGOs believed that it was too early to do anything other than relief. There was evidence to suggest that certain church groups were discouraging people from returning and /or wanted to introduce more camps rather than help disband them. Furthermore, the suggestion that the second report was 'rushed' is also unfounded.

HRW pages 7I and 72: On the question of the numbers of IDPs returning / reintegrating, the one third figure used in the Rogge report was an estimate based on what the NGOs on the ground reported, including the Peace and Justice Commission in Nakuru. The proposal in the Rogge report clearly stated that perhaps as much as a third were back living on their land and about half of the total were cultivating their land but not necessarily living on it, i.e. the other half were displaced.

John Rogge presented these 'numbers' to an NGO seminar on the displaced shortly before his departure and the NGOs present did not disagree with the validity of these assertions. Hence, the UN team used these numbers as working estimates for the programme. It continued to target areas of return or partial return with rehabilitation and recovery projects and areas of displacement with relief and reconciliation activities.

HRW page 77: The statement attributed to the UNDP Administrator, Mr. Speth, in which it suggested that he failed to 'even hint' that there were still problems to be addressed is wrong. In his statement, he clearly made the point that while as many as one-third of the displaced persons had been resettled, there remained many who remained displaced. On page 71, the HRW's own citation of Mr. Speth's speech quotes him as saying that 'there were still intricate land disputes involving the rest' i.e. the 50 percent who remain displaced.

HRW page 84: This is with reference to the temporary housing structures in Kapsokwony referred to in the citation of Tecla Wanjala. This information is incorrect. The temporary housing structures in Kapsokwony were erected by a church-based NGO which did not participate in the UN programme, the agency in question was trying to regroup displaced persons at this site into a relief camp taking them away from a nearby town where they were temporarily settled and at least marginally self-reliant. That NGO rejected the attempt to discourage this project because it felt that the displaced persons needed relief instead of rehabilitation.

3. Harassment of the Displaced, Relief Workers and Journalists:

UNDP constantly raised these concerns with senior Government officials - both publicly and privately. It also ensured that the issues of concern to the displaced were raised both with the donor representatives in Nairobi and with senior visitors (including ministers) from donor capitals. The UNDP was roundly attacked in public for doing so - by the President himself. The UNDP stood its ground and this was eventually the element that brought the joint program to a halt. Others who protested were similarly treated[3].

The access envisaged under the GOK-UN programme did not include journalists or other observers not engaged in the rehabilitation activities. However, the visit of the Administrator of the UNDP was used to urge the government to open up

---

[3] Baroness Chalker, Minister for Overseas Development of the UK whose criticism was dismissed on account of gender was a case in point.

the areas to these groups. This concern was conveyed to the Government in a letter from the Administrator to the President in October 1994.

4. Fraudulent Land Transfer, Illegal Occupation, Pressured Land Sales and Exchanges:

It is true that the justice and land issue was not resolved. The failure to do so, however, was the responsibility of the Government. Both UNDP and other donors (e.g. Germany) offered repeatedly to provide technical assistance for land registration and the reform process. These offers were not accepted. No donor can impose technical assistance when it is not wanted.

5. Providing a National Forum for all Actors:

This section starts in a relatively positive manner. It noted the open and comprehensive participation in the management of the programme which allowed for the first ever meeting of all concerned partners. In fact it was the key instrument through which UNDP addressed the specific challenge of bringing the Government into dialogue with other partners.

It is interesting to note that this achievement is roundly criticised by the same report on the preceding page[4] . UNDP had been solicited by the communities and by the churches and NGOs working with them to bring the Government into the process. All parties considered this to be appropriate at the time.

The establishment of the NCDP resulted from an initiative of UNDP. The committee could not have existed, however, without the agreement of the Government of Kenya to participate and to assume its responsibilities. Again all involved considered the full participation of the Government as the key to the success of the operation, and that Government chairmanship was an appropriate means of obtaining its public commitment to all the goals of the programme.

6. No Comprehensive Data Collection:

On page 68 and elsewhere references are made to the inadequacy of data collection. IDP data are notoriously difficult to pin down. Undertaking a detailed enumeration can actually place people at risk. Many of the IDPs did not want to be on 'lists'. Many were dispersed among relatives or even out of the region and hence could never be sampled even if the UNDMT had tried.

The estimates throughout were just that - estimates. This was made abundantly clear in both Rogge reports and UNDP had always indicated that the 250,000 figure that was being used was little more than a crude estimate. The number

---

[4] The assertion that the UN has assisted a programme that was blatantly manipulated by the Government to further its own ends is a very one-sided interpretation of a complex situation.

was, however, based exclusively on data provided to Rogge by the NGOs and Churches; at no time were any Government estimates used.

Rogge spent over three days in the field with the very person who is cited as having made this allegation. The figures on IDPs in the Nakuru area which were used in his report were derived from the Nakuru based Justice and Peace Foundation. The suggestion therefore, that Rogge 'threw out figures' is misleading. All the data on IDP numbers cited in the report, which formed the basis for the UN programme, were obtained from local churches and NGOs.

HRW page 70: The specific reference to the Rogge report underestimating numbers by 30,000 was explained at a meeting with the HRW in New York in February. This explanation has not been taken into consideration in the current report. The issue concerned data for Mt. Elgon region where the NCCK had greatly inflated numbers. Rogge opted on the side of caution to adjust these numbers to what he saw on the ground. He was subsequently proved right in doing this since two months after the survey the NCCK Relief Co-ordinator for the Mt. Elgon area was removed for misappropriating relief funds and was accused of greatly inflating the number of beneficiaries in his area.

The missing 30,000 to which the HRW refers in report are the 30,000 which the NCCK Co-ordinator was accused of inflating. A more basic issue is that given the uncertainties of the data, to dwell extensively on whether the numbers were 250,000 or 280,000 is somewhat irrelevant.

7. No Terms of Agreement with Government / Government Undermining of the UNDP Program:

The proposals of the NCDP for a continued and expanded programme were duly transmitted to the Government in writing as the basis for formulation of a new phase of activities. At the same time they were incorporated into the basic agreement between the Government and UNDP.

The UN team on the ground, including the UNDP Resident Representative would agree that the lack of a formal agreement between UNDP and the Government has been criticised as one of the factors contributing to the confusion. This confusion arose, in part, from the difficulty in reaching agreement with the Government, but also the uncertainty over funding that made it impossible for UNDP to enter into specific commitments that would have allowed it to call for reciprocal formal commitments from the Government.

A formal financing agreement would have obliged the donors to prioritise the interest of the victims of ethnic violence above their overall aid policy in Kenya similar to the humanitarian relief for drought victims in 1992-93.

6. Reluctance to Criticise Government Human Rights Abuses:

The issue of IDPs in the Rift Valley and Western Kenya was important for
donors from 1993 to 1995, but it was not the determining factor in decisions on
aid and investment. Structural Adjustment was the priority.

This was the critical aspect of the Kenyan situation discussed at the Consultative
Group meeting of 15 December 1994. The statement of Chair of that meeting, in
voicing the generally accepted view that there had been improvements in the
human rights area as well as a lessening of ethnic tension, contributed to the
decision to release external funding but it did not determine it. The sudden
reversal of budgetary policy that occurred in the week following the CG meeting
was a more serious development for most donors than the tragedy at Maela. It
was certainly the key factor that led to a change of heart on the part of the World
Bank and the IMF.

9. No Protection Component / Inadequate Security or Protection:

The UN programme for IDPs, co-ordinated by the Resident Co-ordinator and
UNDMT, and implemented through a UNDP project, had two primary objectives,
namely:

(a) work towards attenuating the escalating political violence through the
physical presence in affected regions of UN field personnel and through behind-
the-scenes negotiations by the UN Resident Co-ordinator with senior
Government officials;

(b) start laying the foundations for the eventual resolution of the conflict by
facilitating the gradual return of most IDPs.

At no time did the UNDMT, the RC, or UNDP imply that it had the capacity or
mandate to become the primary advocate against human rights violations in
Kenya.

Much of the criticism of UNDP contained in the HRW report is basically a
misinformed commentary on UNDP's 'failure' to be the international human rights
monitor, arbitrator and advocate in Kenya during the crisis. This indicates
HRW's misunderstanding of UNDP's role and its limitations to engaging in
'sovereign' issues for which it has no mandate. Instead of blaming UNDP for not
solving the human rights problems in Kenya, the report should identify the link
between human rights violations and the policy of the Government at that time.

10. Strained Relationship with Donors:

UNDP used the NCDP and other mechanisms to keep donors fully informed.
During the preparatory phase, Resident Representatives had regularly briefed

the aid representatives of the development of the proposed programme, based on the Rogge report which was made available to all.

In addition, contrary to the assertions of the HRW report, the UN team worked closely with representatives of NCDP and other interested members of the diplomatic community who offered to take responsibility for the more sensitive interventions. Several leading diplomats posted in Kenya advised the Resident Co-ordinator to continue the quiet diplomacy, leaving direct interventions and public criticism of the Government to them.

11. Abandoning the Displaced:

The UN programme was not suspended as the draft report indicates. It ended in November, with a Government agreement in principle to incorporate activities in favour of displaced persons in its social dimensions of development programme.

28 April 1997